BIG LITTLE
FELT
UNIVERSE

BIG LITTLE
FELT
UNIVERSE

Sew It, Stuff It, Squeeze It, Fun!

Jeanette Lim

LARK CRAFTS

An Imprint of Sterling Publishing Co., Inc.
New York

WWW.LARKCRAFTS.COM

EDITOR: **LINDA KOPP**
ART DIRECTOR: **KRISTI PFEFFER**
ILLUSTRATOR: **ORRIN LUNDGREN**
PHOTOGRAPHER: **STEVE MANN**
STEP-BY-STEP PHOTOGRAPHER: **JEANETTE LIM**
COVER DESIGNER: **KRISTI PFEFFER**

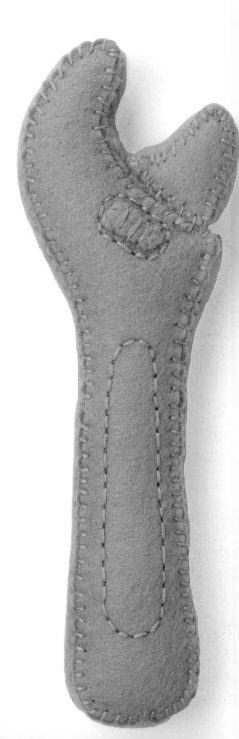

Library of Congress Cataloging-in-Publication Data

Lim, Jeanette.
  Big little felt universe : sew it, stuff it, squeeze it, fun! / Jeanette Lim. -- 1st ed.
    p. cm.
  Includes index.
  ISBN 978-1-60059-675-9 (pb-trade pbk. : alk. paper)
  1. Felt work. I. Title.
  TT849.5.L56 2011
  746'.0463--dc22

                                2010020679

10 9 8 7 6 5 4 3 2 1

First Edition

Published by Lark Crafts, An Imprint of
Sterling Publishing Co., Inc.
387 Park Avenue South, New York, NY 10016

Text © 2011, Jeanette Lim
Project photography © 2011, Lark Crafts, an Imprint of Sterling Publishing Co., Inc.,
unless otherwise specified
Step-by-step photography © 2011, Jeanette Lim
Illustrations © 2011, Lark Crafts, an Imprint of Sterling Publishing Co., Inc.,
unless otherwise specified

Distributed in Canada by Sterling Publishing,
c/o Canadian Manda Group, 165 Dufferin Street
Toronto, Ontario, Canada M6K 3H6

Distributed in the United Kingdom by GMC Distribution Services,
Castle Place, 166 High Street, Lewes, East Sussex, England BN7 1XU

Distributed in Australia by Capricorn Link (Australia) Pty Ltd.,
P.O. Box 704, Windsor, NSW 2756 Australia

If you have questions or comments about this book, please contact:
Lark Crafts
67 Broadway
Asheville, NC 28801
828-253-0467

Manufactured in China

ISBN 13: 978-1-60059-675-9

For information about custom editions, special sales, premium and corporate
purchases, please contact Sterling Special Sales Department at 800-805-5489 or
specialsales@sterlingpub.com.

For information about desk and examination copies available to college and
university professors, requests must be submitted to academic@larkbooks.com.
Our complete policy can be found at www.larkcrafts.com.

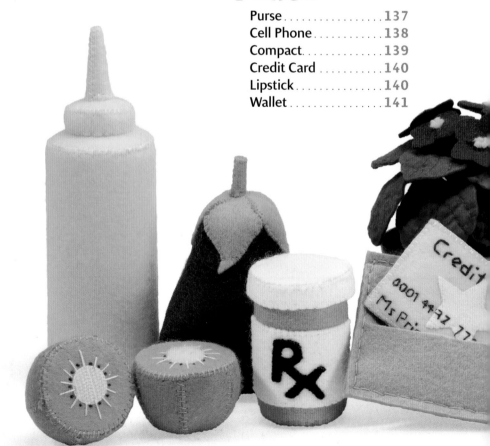

contents

Welcome ✱ ようこそ ✱ Bienvenue ✱ Bienvenido ✱ Willkommen
to BIG LITTLE FELT UNIVERSE,
where there's something fun for everyone.

Grill it, grow it, fix it, buy it

Slice it, ice it, build it, try it!

It's the good life, in felt, and it's time to play.
What will you make today?

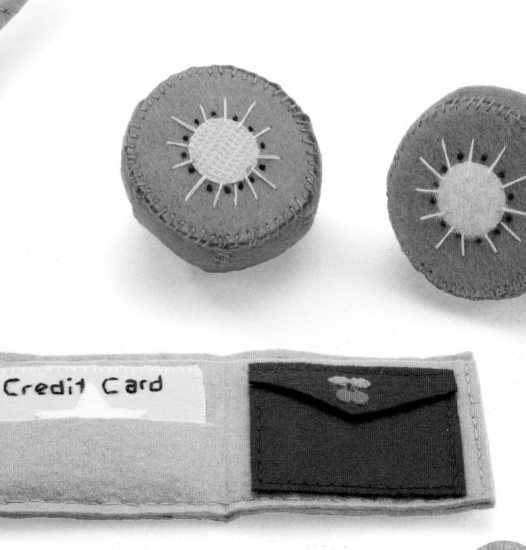

Credit Card

f. y. i.

One of the joys of making the projects in this book is that you don't need a lot of stuff. More happiness is that they're fun and easy. So after reading the next few pages, you'll know what materials to get and what you need to know to get started, and then you'll be all set for some feltie fun!

SUPPLIES

The materials listed below are used in all the projects, so you'll need to gather them before you begin. You probably have a lot of them already, and what you don't have won't cost you a bundle. You'll find a complete listing of the tools and materials needed for each felt set at the end of the project chapter, located with the patterns.

Felt

Not all felt is created equally. As a felt pattern designer, I've tried many different types. I find acrylic craft felt (made from a polyester blend of fibers) pulls at the stitches and can rip if you overstuff your item, while 100 percent wool felt is too thick. So I use 1 mm-thick wool blend felt. It's a bit more expensive than the acrylic kind but much more durable, and you'll want your feltie to hold up to lots of squeezing. If you're making something for a wee one, make sure the felt is baby/child safe.

You can purchase wool blend felt online and in some craft stores. I use Sunfelt felt (from Japan); the colors marked on each pattern piece is how the company identifies its colors, but the names are also descriptive and will assist you when choosing any brand of felt.

Scissors

Fabric scissors for cutting felt fabrics (make sure they're sharp!)
Paper scissors for cutting cardboard and other materials
Eyebrow scissors for snipping and cutting tiny pieces

Sewing Needles

No particular length or thickness is required. All the projects are 100 percent hand-sewn, so use whatever works best for you.

Sewing Thread

Nothing fancy, use standard 60-weight sewing threads that are typically used for sewing by hand or machine. Choose colors that closely match those of your felt fabrics.

Ruler

For the most accurate measurements, make sure you have one that shows centimeters; many of them do. In a few instances, a pattern was too large to run at actual size so I've indicated the measurements on the pattern. Just measure and draw the lengths onto your felt.

Pencils & Markers

Use a #2 pencil for most light fabrics. For darker fabrics such as black and brown, use a 0.5 white color marker pen or chalk pencil.

Stuffing

Fiberfill or polyfill works best for maximum fluffiness. Cotton stuffing makes the item lumpy (not a good look) and will not go back into shape like fiberfill does when pressed.

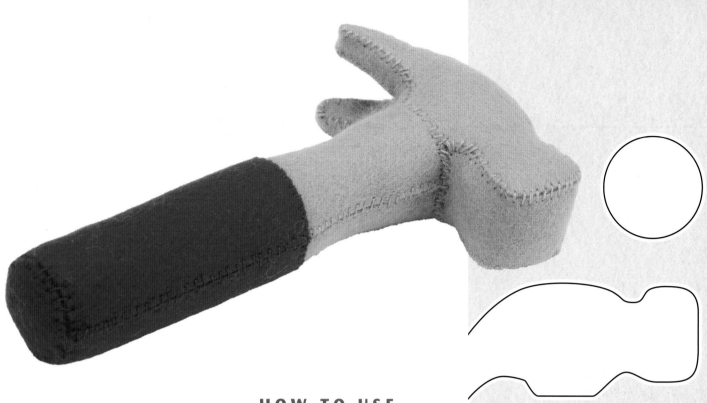

OTHER MATERIALS

Some of the felties require a few additional materials other than the ones just listed. Be sure to check the Supplies list for each project to determine exactly what you'll need.

Nylon thread

Non-toxic quick dry craft glue

Metal sheets
(available at craft stores)

Magnet buttons

Aluminum wire

Cardboard/posterboard
(purchase at craft stores or use the cardboard from packaged grocery items like cereal boxes)

PVC plastic sheet
(you can buy this at craft stores or use the clear report covers found at office supply stores.)

Long tweezers or a chopstick

Wire/metal sheet cutter

Felt ribbon

Cellophane tape

HOW TO USE THE PATTERNS IN THIS BOOK

Most of the patterns are shown at actual size so they require no pesky enlarging. In the rare cases where a pattern is marked with ✱, measure and cut the felt pieces according to the measurements given on the pattern piece. Not to worry, these pattern pieces are all simple squares or rectangles.

Photocopy or trace each pattern piece onto paper and then cut it out. Trace the pattern onto your felt. Once you've cut out your felt pieces, leave the paper patterns on top of them for easy identification.

WHIP STITCH

BLANKET STITCH

BACKSTITCH

FRENCH KNOT

STRAIGHT STITCH

STITCHES USED

Just five simple stitches were used to make the projects in this book. Unless otherwise stated in the instructions, the default stitch is always the Whip Stitch.

Whip Stitch

Whip Stitch is the most commonly used stitch. It's perfect for sewing two pieces of felt fabric together in order to create round shapes. It's normally used with thread color that matches your felt so an advantage is any uneven stitches won't be very obvious.

Blanket Stitch

Blanket Stitch is used mostly on flat edges to neaten them. It can also be used as a decorative stitch using different colored thread, but you'll need to make sure your stitches are even.

Backstitch

Back Stitch is used to define details and to outline shapes.

French Knot

French Knots are usually used to define details and outline shapes.

Straight Stitch

Straight Stitch (aka Running Stitch) is actually individual stitches sewn without crossing or looping the thread. It looks like a broken line. It's easily removable and thus sometimes used to tack two pieces of fabric together temporarily.

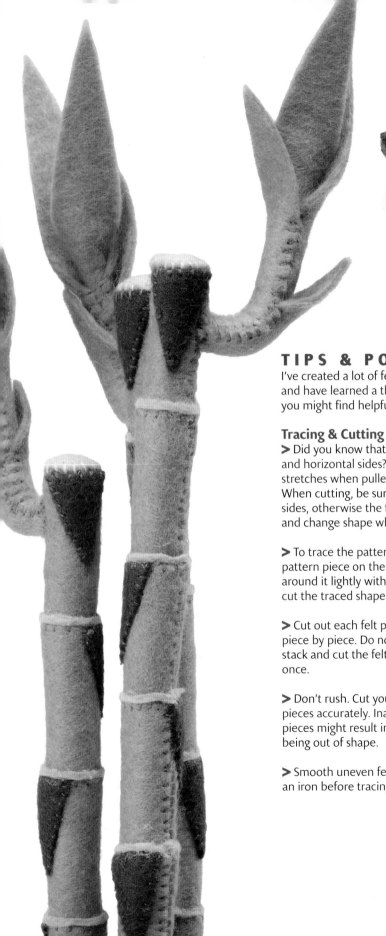

TIPS & POINTERS

I've created a lot of felties over time and have learned a thing or two that you might find helpful.

Tracing & Cutting

> Did you know that felt has vertical and horizontal sides? The side that stretches when pulled is horizontal. When cutting, be sure to match the sides, otherwise the felt may stretch and change shape when stuffed.

> To trace the patterns, place a pattern piece on the felt, trace around it lightly with a pencil, and cut the traced shape out.

> Cut out each felt pattern lovingly piece by piece. Do not attempt to stack and cut the felt together at once.

> Don't rush. Cut your felt pattern pieces accurately. Inaccurate felt pieces might result in the final item being out of shape.

> Smooth uneven felt surfaces with an iron before tracing and cutting.

Sewing

> For sewing and attaching pieces together, choose a thread color similar to that of your felt and work with double strands of thread. This makes for stronger, cleaner stitches.

> When sewing felt pieces together, take care not to pull too hard or the surface will become wavy.

> If you make a mistake and need to resew, you can fill the needle holes by gathering fibers from the surrounding surface area using the tip of a needle.

Stuffing

> Stuff the item bit by bit, filling up the sides first, then the center.

> Use tweezers or a stick to stuff smaller parts where your fingers can't reach.

Cleaning & Washing

> Wool blend felt can be washed. Although it can be machine washed, I'd recommend handwashing your feltie. Be aware that the piece will shrink about 10 percent.

> You can spot clean a feltie using cellophane tape. Rub the adhesive side over the surface to remove any unwanted markings or fibers.

CAKE

One slice, two slice,
fruit cake is oh so nice.

CAKE

1. Tape the **cardboard** Cake Top, Base, Side, and Back together.

2. Sew the Cake Center pieces to the Cake Side.

3. Stitch the Cake Top and Base to the Cake Side, then sew the Cake Back to the Top, leaving an opening as shown.

4. Insert the **cardboard** form into the cake, fill with stuffing, and sew the opening closed. Repeat the same for the other five slices.

5. Place eight Whipped Cream pieces together as shown.

6. Turn the stack over, pinch the straight side together, and over stitch using WHITE thread.

7. Turn the piece over and spread out the Whipped Cream evenly.

8. Repeat steps 5 through 7 for the remaining 17 Whipped Creams. Sew three Whipped Creams to the edge of the Cake Slice. Repeat for the other slices.

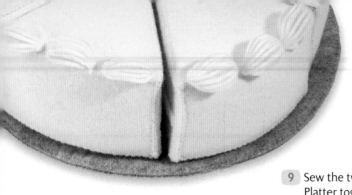

PLATTER

9 Sew the two pieces of the Cake Platter together halfway and then insert the two **cardboard** Cake Platter pieces in between. Stitch up the opening.

PEACH

10 Sew the Peach Side and End together, filling with stuffing. Repeat for the rest of the Peach Slices.

ORANGE

11 Stitch the details onto the Orange Slice as shown.

12 Stitch two Orange Slices together, filling with stuffing. Repeat for the rest of the Orange Slices.

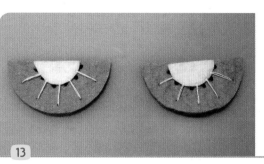

13 Sew the Kiwi Center onto the Kiwi Slice and stitch on the details as shown.

14 Sandwich a Kiwi Side between two Kiwi Slices and stitch together, filling with stuffing. Repeat for the rest of the Kiwi Slices.

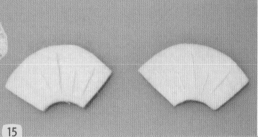

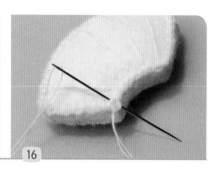

PINEAPPLE

15 Stitch the details on the Pineapple Slices as shown.

16 Sandwich a Pineapple Side between two Pineapple Slices and stitch together, filling with stuffing. Repeat for the rest of the Pineapple Slices.

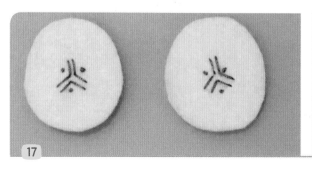

BANANA

17 Stitch the details on the Banana Slice as shown.

18 Sandwich a Banana Side between two Banana Slices and stitch together, filling with stuffing. Repeat for the rest of the Bananas.

CAKE

19 Attach the Strawberry Center to the Slice and stitch the details as shown. Sew the Side between two Slices, filling with stuffing. Repeat for the rest of the Strawberries.

STRAWBERRY

RASPBERRY

20 Stitch around the edge of the Raspberry, leaving the thread ends loose.

21 Pull both ends of the threads, fill with stuffing, and fasten the thread ends with knots. Trim away the excess threads.

22 Sew vertical lines on the Raspberry.

23 Sew horizontal lines.

24 Sew the Base to the Raspberry, covering the opening. Repeat for the rest of the raspberries.

BLUEBERRY

25 Cut the "X" on the Blueberry and glue the Blueberry center on top.

26 Repeat steps 20 and 21 for the Blueberry.

27 Sew the Base to the Blueberry, covering the opening. Repeat the same for the rest of the Blueberries.

CAKE

CANDLES

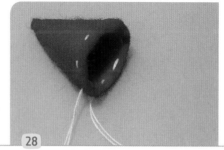

28

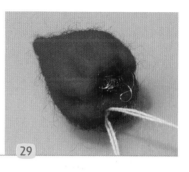

29

30

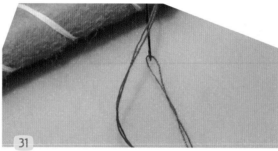

31

32

28 Sew the side of the Candle Flame together. Stitch around the edge with a running stitch, leaving the thread ends loose.

29 Fill the Flame with stuffing and then pull and tie both ends of the threads together. Trim off the excess threads.

30 Roll up the Candle (on the longer side), and twirl white thread around it as shown.

31 Stitch the Flame onto the Candle.

32 Sew the hook-and-loop Candle Base to the bottom of the Candle. Repeat steps 28 through 32 for the rest of the Candles.

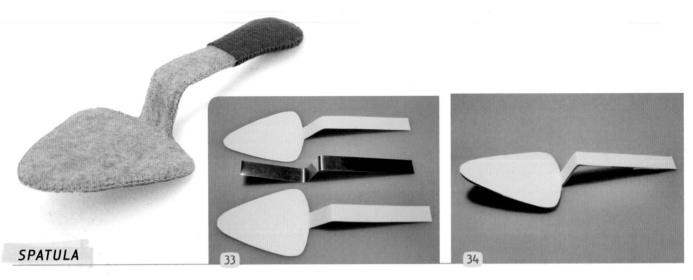

SPATULA

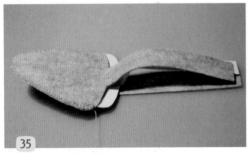
33

33

34

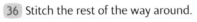
35

36

37

33 Fold both the **cardboard** and **metal sheet** Cake Spatula on the lines indicated on the pattern.

34 Tape the Spatula pieces together with the metal sheet sandwiched in between the cardboard.

35 Sew the front part of the two felt Spatula pieces together, inserting the cardboard form in between.

36 Stitch the rest of the way around.

37 Sew the Handles to the Spatula.

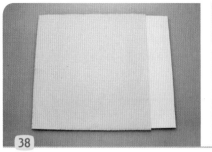

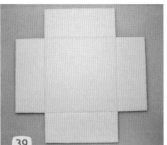

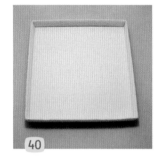

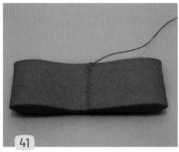

38 Sew three sides of the Cake Box Base together, then insert the cardboard Cake Box Base and stitch the opening closed.

39 Repeat the previous step to make the Cake Box Base Sides. Sew them together as shown.

40 Repeat steps 38 and 39, substituting the Cake Box Top pieces for the Cake Box Base pieces. Fold the Box Top Sides up and stitch at the corners.

41 Sew the ends of the Ribbon Bow Layer 1 together and flatten it such that the stitches are at the center as shown. Repeat with the other piece.

42 Turn each Ribbon Bow Layer 1 over and stitch the center together as shown. Repeat steps 41 and 42 for the Ribbon Bow Layer 2 pieces.

43 Sew the Bow pieces together at the center as shown.

44 Sew the sides of the Ribbon Bow Center together and flatten it down.

45 Assemble and sew all the Ribbon Bow pieces together as shown.

46 Glue the Ribbon on top of the Cake Box cover as shown.

47 Glue the Ribbon Bow at the center.

FADED GRAY
15¾" x 15¾" (40cm x 40cm)

LIGHT PINK
15¾" x 15¾" (40cm x 40cm),
5 pieces

DEEP PINK
12" x 8" (30cm x 20cm)

WALNUT BROWN
2½" x 3¼" (6cm x 8cm)

WHITE
15¾" x 15¾" (40cm x 40cm),
2 pieces

CHILI RED
6" x 8" (15cm x 20cm)

SOFT PINK
3¼" x 2½" (8cm x 6cm)

BRIGHT YELLOW
3¼" x 2½" (8cm x 6cm)

SKY BLUE
3¼" x 2½" (8cm x 6cm)

LIGHT PURPLE
3¼" x 3¼" (8cm x 8cm)

ORANGE
8" x 8" (20cm x 20cm)

LIGHT GREEN
3¼" x 2½" (8cm x 6cm)

LEAF GREEN
6" x 8" (15cm x 20cm)

LEMON FROST
15¾" x 15¾" (40cm x 40cm)

YELLOW
4" x 8" (10cm x 20cm)

DARK PURPLE
4" x 4¾" (10cm x 12cm)

CHERRY RED
4" x 4¾" (10cm x 12cm)

1mm-thick cardboard
23¼" x 16½" (59cm x 42cm),
5 pieces

0.008 tin sheet metal
¾" x 6¼" (2cm x 16cm)

White hook-and-loop fastener
¾" x 3¼" (2cm x 8cm)

Wire cutters

Non-toxic craft glue

Cellophane tape

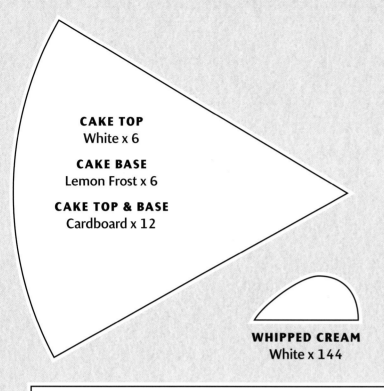

CAKE TOP
White x 6

CAKE BASE
Lemon Frost x 6

CAKE TOP & BASE
Cardboard x 12

CAKE BACK
White x 6
Cardboard x 6

WHIPPED CREAM
White x 144

CAKE SIDE
Lemon Frost x 6

CAKE SIDE
Cardboard x 6

CAKE CENTER
White x 6

CAKE CENTER
White x 6

CAKE PLATTER
Faded Gray x 2 (outer circle)
Cardboard x 2 (inner circle)

CAKE

KIWI SLICE
Leaf Green x 12

KIWI CENTER
White x 12

PINEAPPLE SLICE
Lemon Frost x 12

KIWI SIDE
Leaf green x 6

PINEAPPLE SIDE
Lemon Frost x 6

STRAWBERRY SLICE
Chili Red x 12

STRAWBERRY CENTER
White x 12

BANANA SLICE
Lemon Frost x 12

STRAWBERRY SIDE
Chilli Red x 6

BANANA SIDE
Lemon Frost x 6

BLUEBERRY CENTER
Light Purple x 6

BLUEBERRY BASE
Dark Purple x 6

RASPBERRY BASE
Cherry Red x 6

BLUEBERRY
Dark Purple x 6

RASPBERRY
Cherry Red x 6

PEACH END
Yellow x 6

PEACH SIDE
Yellow x 12

ORANGE SLICE
Orange x 12

CAKE

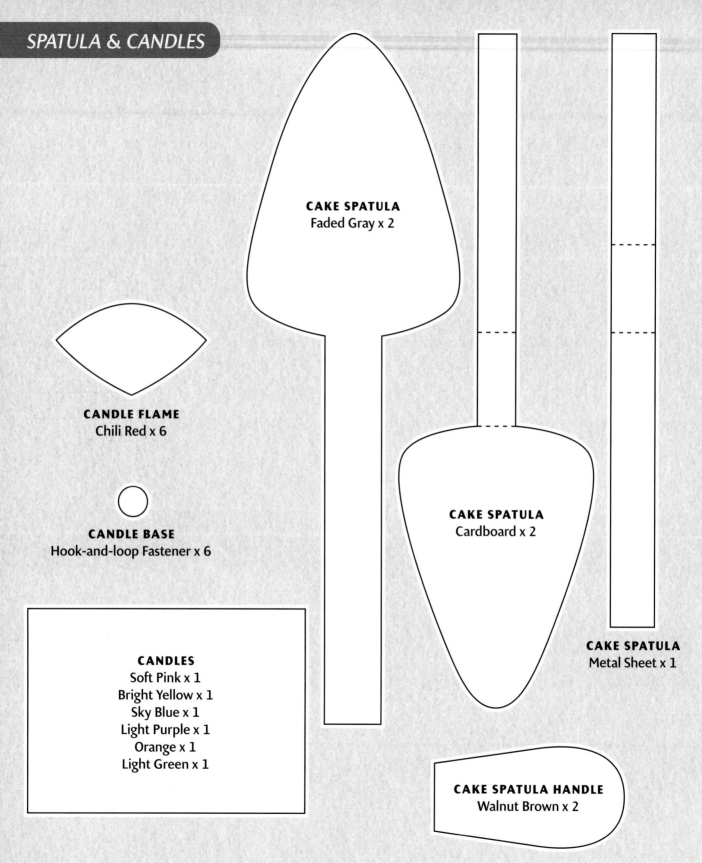

CAKE SPATULA
Faded Gray x 2

CANDLE FLAME
Chili Red x 6

CANDLE BASE
Hook-and-loop Fastener x 6

CANDLES
Soft Pink x 1
Bright Yellow x 1
Sky Blue x 1
Light Purple x 1
Orange x 1
Light Green x 1

CAKE SPATULA
Cardboard x 2

CAKE SPATULA
Metal Sheet x 1

CAKE SPATULA HANDLE
Walnut Brown x 2

*Cut out according to measurements stated

*CAKE BOX TOP
Light Pink x 2
9" x 9" (22.5cm x 22.5cm)

*CAKE BOX BASE
Light Pink x 2
8¾" x 8¾" (22cm x 22cm)

*CAKE BOX BASE SIDES
Light Pink x 8
9" x 3½" (22.5cm x 9cm)

*CAKE BOX BASE SIDES
Cardboard x 4
8¾" x 3¼" (22cm x 8.5cm)

*CAKE BOX TOP SIDES
Light Pink x 8
8½" x 1" (21.5cm x 2.5cm)

*CAKE BOX TOP & BASE
Cardboard x 2
8½" x 8½"
(21.5cm x 21.5cm)

*CAKE BOX TOP SIDES
Cardboard x 4
8¼" x ¾" (21cm x 2cm)

*RIBBON
Deep Pink x 2
11" x 1¼" (28cm x 3cm)

*RIBBON BOW CENTER
Deep Pink x 1
2¼" x 1" (5.5cm x 2.5cm)

*RIBBON BOW LAYER 1
Deep Pink x 2
8¼" x 1¼" (21cm x 3cm)

*RIBBON BOW LAYER 2
Deep Pink x 2
7" x 1¼" (18cm x 3cm)

CAMPING

Fire roaring, lantern glowing,
compass shows which way we're going.

LOGS

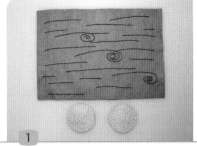

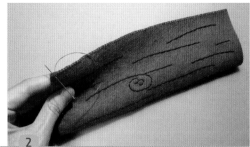

1 Stitch the wood grain details on all of the Log and Log Ends as shown.

2 Sew the sides of the log together.

3 Sew one Log End on.

4 Sew on the other Log End, leaving an opening for stuffing.

5 Fill the log with stuffing and stitch up the opening.

6 Repeat steps 1 through 5 for the other two logs.

FIRE

7 Sew the Inner, Middle, and Outer Zones of the fire together as shown.

8 Repeat the previous step two more times.

9 Apply glue generously to the backs of the fire pieces.

10 Glue the backs of the fire together as shown.

11 Stitch the edges of the fire with a blanket stitch, and leave to dry.

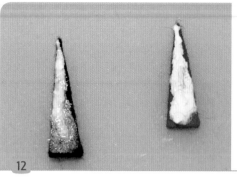

12 To stiffen the felt, apply glue to the backs of the Compass Needles and leave to dry.

13 Stitch the details onto the Compass Top as shown.

14 Sew the Compass Side and Compass Base together.

15 Insert a **cardboard** Compass Base into the bottom of the compass.

16 Sew the Compass Top on halfway.

17 Fill the compass with stuffing, insert the other **cardboard** Base on top of the stuffing, and stitch the opening closed.

18 Sew down through the Compass Center into the ends of the red then the black Compass Needles, and straight through the center of the Compass Top as shown.

19 Sew the compass together.

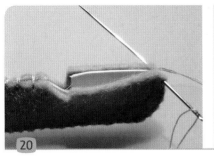

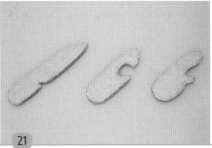

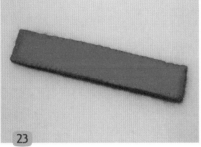

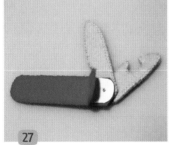

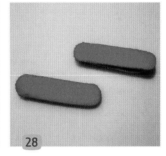

20 Place the **cardboard** Blade in between the two felt Blade pieces and sew them together.

21 Repeat step 20 for the Bottle Opener and the Can Opener/Screwdriver.

22 Sew three-quarters of the way around the felt Casing pieces, then insert the **cardboard** Casing pieces as shown. Set them aside.

23 Sew the two felt Casing Base pieces together with the **cardboard** Casing in between.

24 Fold back the felt and stitch the Can Opener to one of the Casings at the unsewn end, as shown (see next photo for details).

25 Poke your needle through the cardboard Casing and stitch the Can Opener to only the **cardboard**. Tie a few knots to fasten the stitch.

26 Stitch the Blade and Bottle Opener to the other Casing using the same method as above.

27 Tie a few knots to make sure the stitches are fastened to the **cardboard**.

28 Sew the openings on both casings closed.

29 Sandwich the **cardboard** Casing Base between the two felt Casing Base pieces and stitch the piece to the casing, curving the piece as you go.

LANTERN

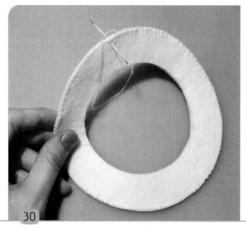
30

31

32

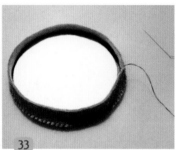
33

34

35

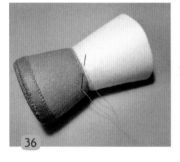
36

37

38

39

30 Sew the outside edge of the two Collar pieces together with a blanket stitch.

31 Sew the sides of the Outer and Inner Stand pieces together.

32 Sew the Stand Border and Stand Base together.

33 Place the **cardboard** Stand Base inside the stand.

34 Insert the Stand inside the Base, and sew them together as shown.

35 Fill the Stand with stuffing, and sew the Stand Top on.

36 Sew the sides of the Inner and Outer Screen together, and stitch it to the stand as shown.

37 Sew the Lamp Border on.

38 Sew the Cap Base and Cap Side together. Stitch the Cap Top on halfway and insert a **cardboard** Cap piece as shown.

39 Fill the cap with stuffing, and insert the other **cardboard** Cap piece on top of the stuffing.

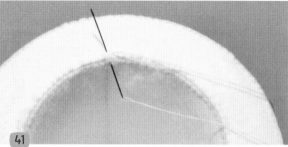

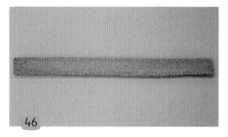

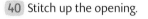

40 Stitch up the opening.

41 Sew the inner part of the Collar to the Top of the Screen.

42 Fill the Screen with stuffing.

43 Sew the Cap on.

44 Sew the Top, Base, and Side of the Control Knob together, leaving an opening for stuffing. Stuff and finish sewing together.

45 Sew the Control Knob onto the base as shown.

46 Sew the edges of the two Handle pieces together using a blanket stitch.

47 Sew the Handle to the Cap.

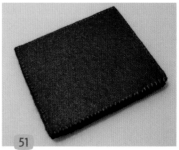

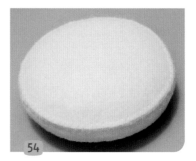

48 Stack three Graham Cracker pieces and sew three of the sides together. Sew French knots on the cracker as shown. Repeat the same process to make the other cracker.

49 Sew the Chocolate Bar Sides to one piece of the Chocolate Bar.

50 Place two Chocolate Bar pieces inside as shown.

51 Place the last piece on top and sew the sides together.

52 Sew the Marshmallow Top, Base, and Side together, leaving an opening.

53 Fill the marshmallow with stuffing.

54 Sew up the opening. Stack the marshmallow and chocolate bar in between the graham crackers.

PEACOCK BLUE
10" x 12" (25cm x 30cm)

DARK GRAY
6" x 10¼" (15cm x 26cm)

IVORY
11" x 13¾" (28cm x 35cm)

CHILI RED
15¾" x 15¾" & 10" x 8"
(40cm x 40cm & 25cm x 20cm)

GRAY
3¼" x 4" (8cm x 10cm)

CHESTNUT BROWN
12½" x 15¾" (32cm x 40cm)

NUTMEG
7" x 7" (18cm x 18cm)

TOMATO RED
12½" x 12½" (32cm x 32cm)

YELLOW
4¾" x 12" (12cm x 30cm)

BLACK
¾" x ¾" (2cm x 2cm)

BLUE
3¼" x 6" (8cm x 15cm)

WHITE
8¾" x 4¾" (22cm x 12cm)

GINGERBREAD
9½" x 6¼" (24cm x 16cm)

COCOA BROWN
6¼" x 4¾" (16cm x 12cm)

1mm-thick cardboard
11½" x 8¼" (29cm x 21cm)

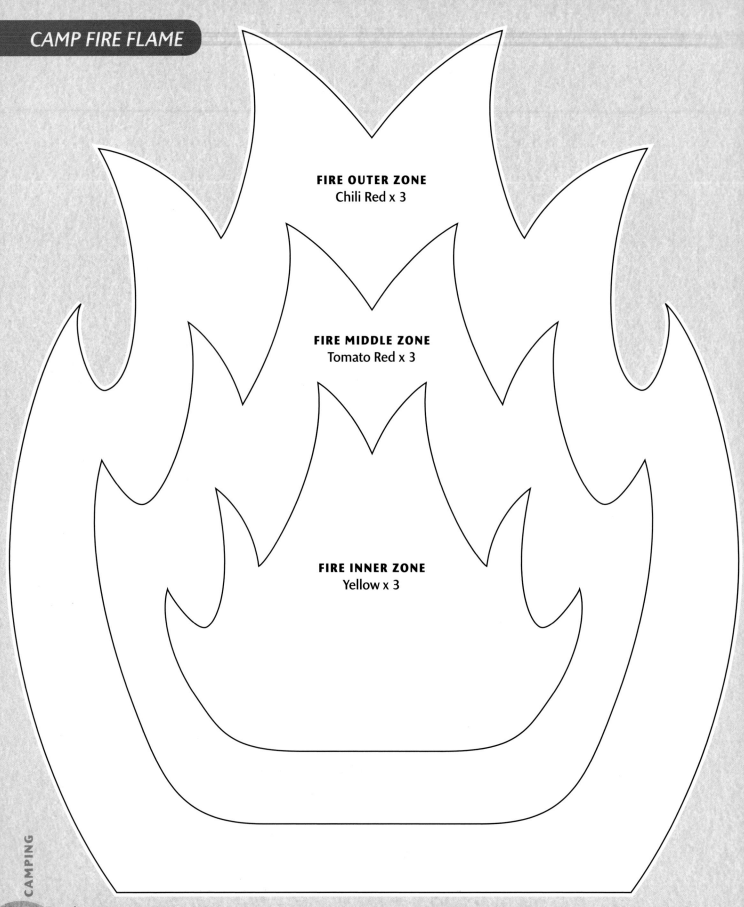

FIRE OUTER ZONE
Chili Red x 3

FIRE MIDDLE ZONE
Tomato Red x 3

FIRE INNER ZONE
Yellow x 3

* Cut out according to measurements stated

* LOG
Chestnut Brown x 3
9½" x 6¼" (24cm x 16cm)

LOG END
Nutmeg x 6

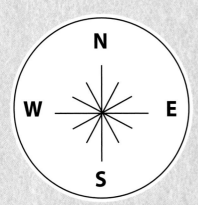

COMPASS TOP & BASE
Blue x 2
White x 1

COMPASS TOP & BASE
Cardboard x 2

COMPASS NEEDLE
Chili Red x 1
Black x 1

COMPASS CENTER
Yellow x 1

COMPASS SIDE
Blue x 1

CAMPING

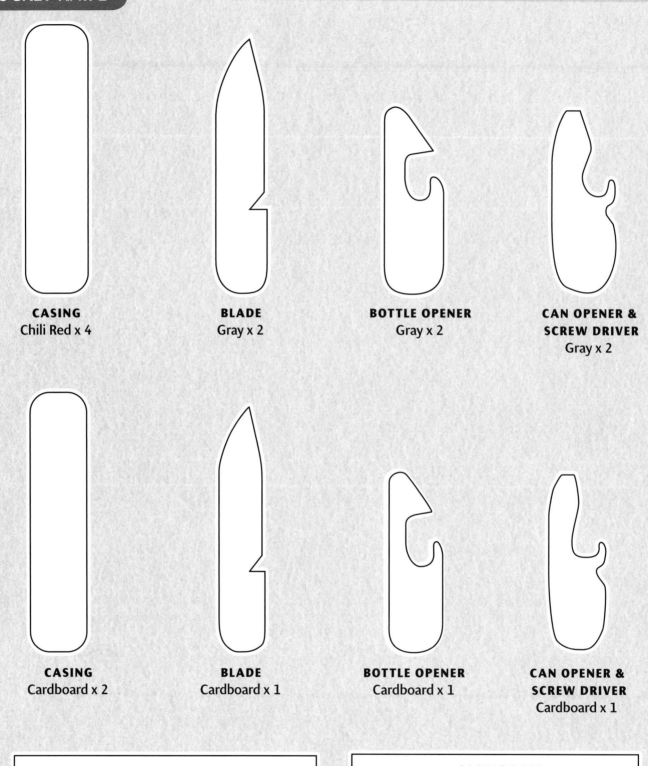

CASING
Chili Red x 4

BLADE
Gray x 2

BOTTLE OPENER
Gray x 2

**CAN OPENER &
SCREW DRIVER**
Gray x 2

CASING
Cardboard x 2

BLADE
Cardboard x 1

BOTTLE OPENER
Cardboard x 1

**CAN OPENER &
SCREW DRIVER**
Cardboard x 1

CASING BASE
Chili Red x 2

CASING BASE
Cardboard x 1

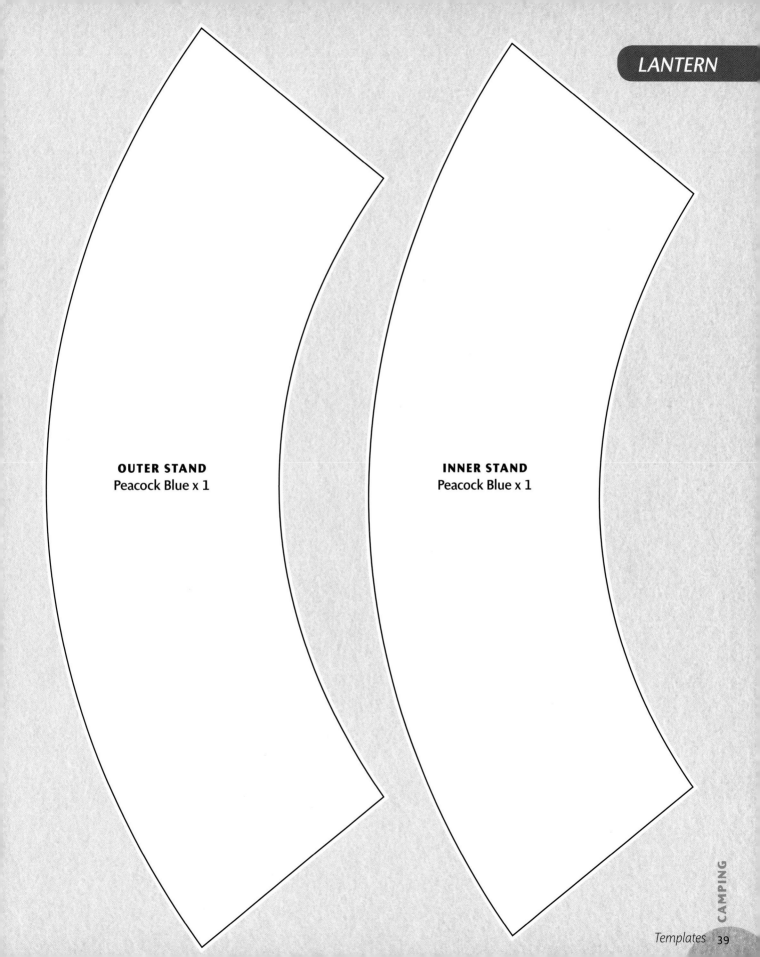

OUTER STAND
Peacock Blue x 1

INNER STAND
Peacock Blue x 1

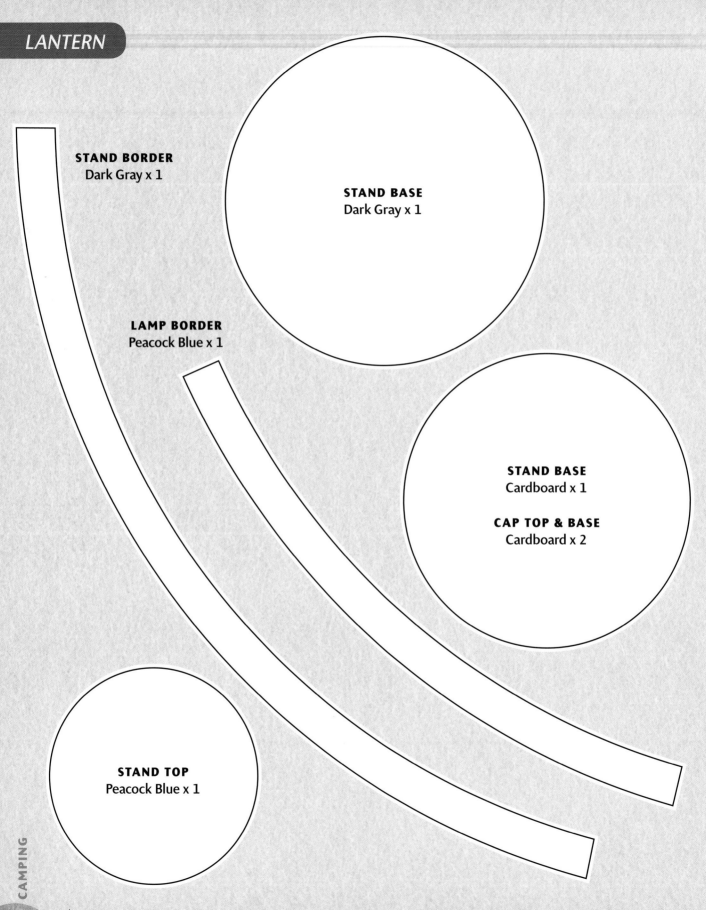

STAND BORDER
Dark Gray x 1

STAND BASE
Dark Gray x 1

LAMP BORDER
Peacock Blue x 1

STAND BASE
Cardboard x 1

CAP TOP & BASE
Cardboard x 2

STAND TOP
Peacock Blue x 1

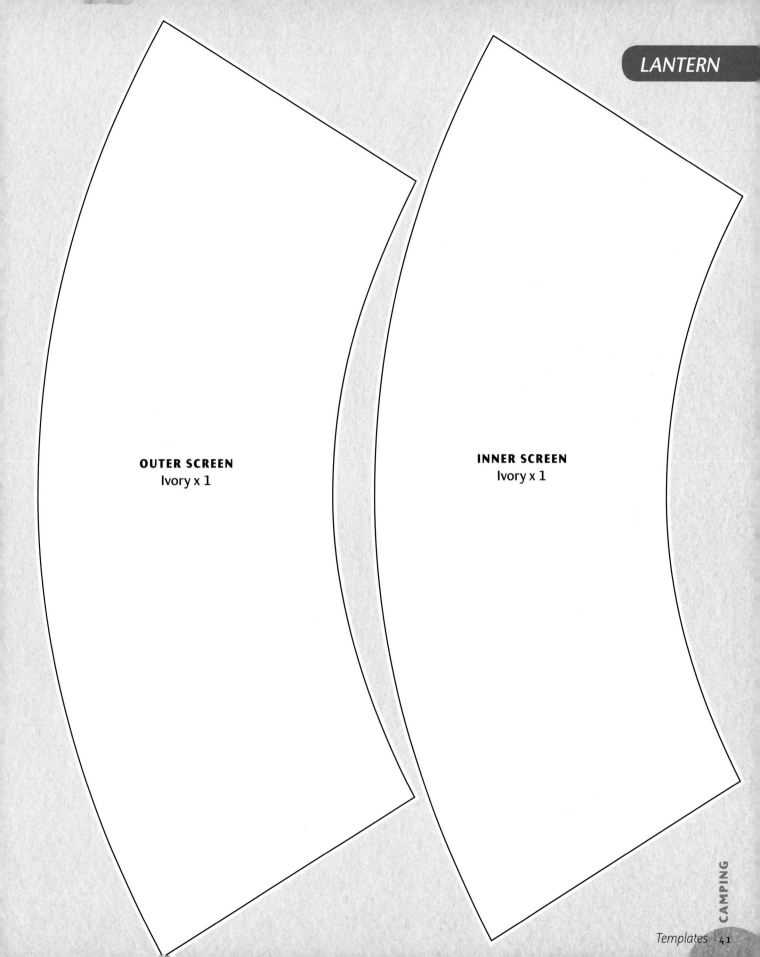

OUTER SCREEN
Ivory x 1

INNER SCREEN
Ivory x 1

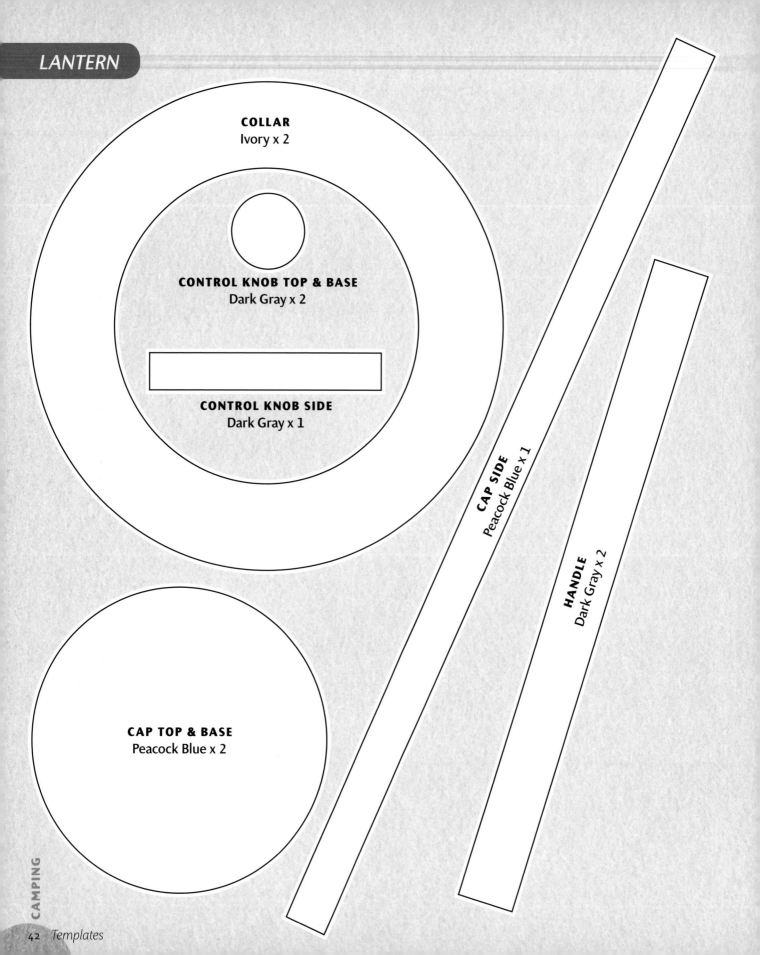

COLLAR
Ivory x 2

CONTROL KNOB TOP & BASE
Dark Gray x 2

CONTROL KNOB SIDE
Dark Gray x 1

CAP SIDE
Peacock Blue x 1

HANDLE
Dark Gray x 2

CAP TOP & BASE
Peacock Blue x 2

GRAHAM CRACKERS
Gingerbread x 6

**MARSHMALLOW
TOP & BASE**
White x 2

CHOCOLATE BAR
Cocoa Brown x 4

MARSHMALLOW SIDE
White x 1

CHOCOLATE BAR SIDE
Cocoa Brown x 2

CAMPING

SUNDAE

Three scoops. Three cheers!
Dieters, have no fear!

BANANA

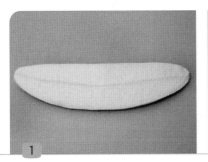

1 Sew the Banana Front Top and Front Bottom together as shown, then stitch on the Banana Back, leaving one long side open for stuffing.

2 Insert the **cardboard** Banana Back Insert at the bottom. Fill with stuffing and stitch the opening closed. Repeat steps 1 and 2 to make the other banana.

ICE CREAM

3 Using a running stitch, sew 2 to 3mm from the edge of the Strawberry Ice Cream, leaving the thread ends loose.

4 Pull both ends of the threads together and fasten the threads with knots.

5 Fill the Ice Cream with stuffing and trim off the excess threads.

6 Stitch the Strawberry Ice Cream Base over the opening.

7 Repeat the same for the Chocolate and Vanilla Ice Cream scoops. Sew the appropriate Syrup onto the top of each Ice Cream as shown.

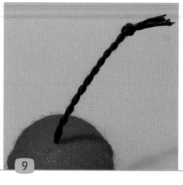

8

9

CHERRY

10

8 Repeat steps 3 through 6 to make the Cherry.

9 Sew about six strands of 1½" (4 cm) long brown threads through the top of the Cherry, then twist and tie a knot at the end as shown.

10 Sew on the Cherry Base.

11

12

WHIPPED CREAM

13

11 Overlap each of the Whipped Cream petals and stitch them together as shown.

12 Flatten the Whipped Cream for the Cherry.

13 Repeat step 11 to make the other two Whipped Cream dollops and then fill them with stuffing.

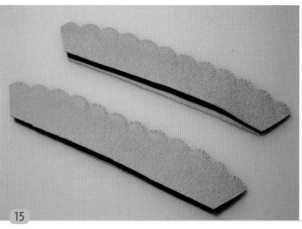

14 Place the **cardboard** Boat Dish Base in between the two felt Boat Dish Base pieces. Sew a couple of stitches to secure the **cardboard** to the sides.

15 Stack two Boat Dish Side pieces and stitch the wavy side with a blanket stitch as shown. Repeat with the other two pieces.

16 Sew the Boat Dish Sides and the Base together.

SOFT GREEN
4¾" x 11½" (12cm x 30cm)

LEMON FROST
4" x 12½" (10cm x 32cm)

IVORY
5" x 7" (13cm x 18cm)

PINK
5" x 7" (13cm x 18cm)

WALNUT BROWN
5" x 7" (13cm x 18cm)

CHERRY RED
2" x 2¾" (5cm x 7cm)

WHITE
6¼" x 6¼" (16cm x 16cm)

BRIGHT YELLOW
3¼" x 3¼" (8cm x 8cm)

CHILI RED
3¼" x 3¼" (8cm x 8cm)

COCOA BROWN
3¼" x 3¼" (8cm x 8cm)

1mm-thick cardboard
8" x 7" (20cm x 18cm)

BANANA BACK
Lemon Frost x 2

BANANA FRONT – TOP
Lemon Frost x 2

BANANA FRONT – BOTTOM
Lemon Frost x 2

BANANA BACK INSERT
Cardboard x 2

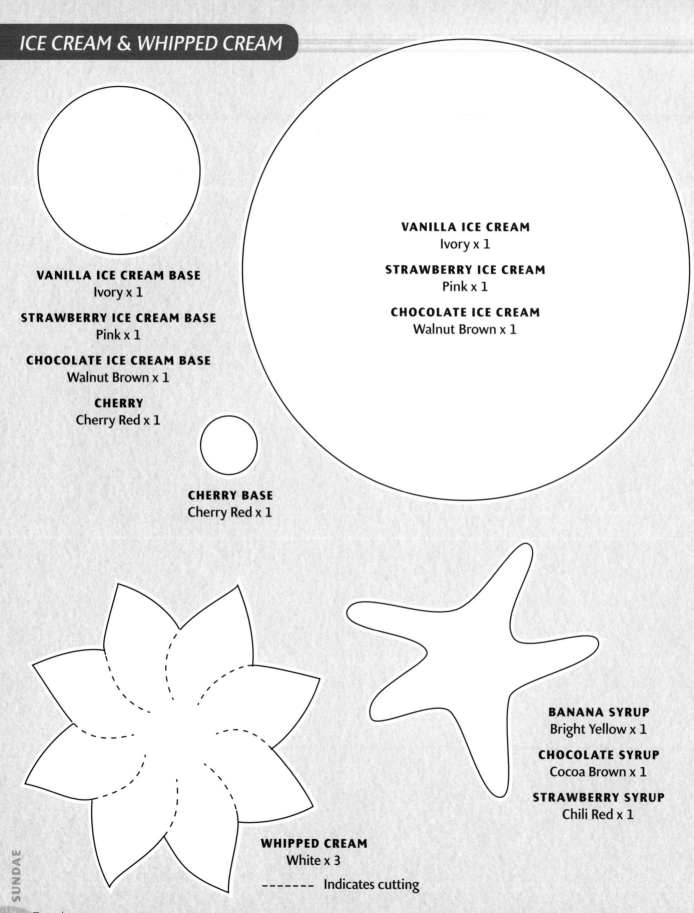

VANILLA ICE CREAM BASE
Ivory x 1

STRAWBERRY ICE CREAM BASE
Pink x 1

CHOCOLATE ICE CREAM BASE
Walnut Brown x 1

CHERRY
Cherry Red x 1

CHERRY BASE
Cherry Red x 1

VANILLA ICE CREAM
Ivory x 1

STRAWBERRY ICE CREAM
Pink x 1

CHOCOLATE ICE CREAM
Walnut Brown x 1

BANANA SYRUP
Bright Yellow x 1

CHOCOLATE SYRUP
Cocoa Brown x 1

STRAWBERRY SYRUP
Chili Red x 1

WHIPPED CREAM
White x 3

------- Indicates cutting

SUNDAE

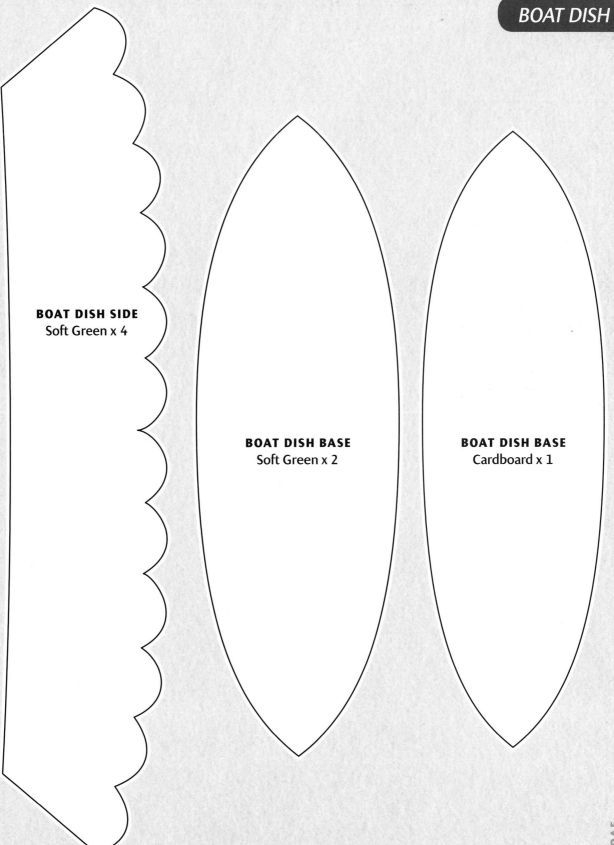

BOAT DISH SIDE
Soft Green x 4

BOAT DISH BASE
Soft Green x 2

BOAT DISH BASE
Cardboard x 1

SUNDAE

OFFICE

No work, all play,
you be the boss today.

CALCULATOR

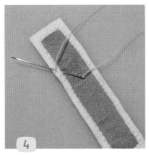

1. Fold where indicated on the pattern, and tape the **cardboard** Front, Back, Side, Top, and Base pieces together as shown.

2. Stitch the Numbers, Letters, and Signs onto the keys as shown.

3. Sew the keys onto the front of the calculator evenly.

4. Sew the Numbers Screen to the Numbers Screen Border.

5. Stitch the Number Screen and Solar Panel onto the calculator.

6. Sew the Back, Sides, and Base to the calculator Front, leaving the top section unsewn.

7. Slide the **cardboard** form into the calculator.

8. Sew the Top of the calculator on.

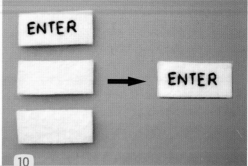

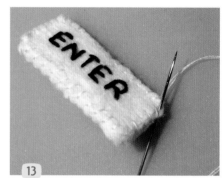

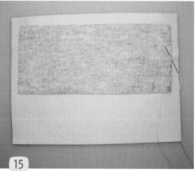

9 Stitch the Numbers and Letters onto the Keys (one piece each).

10 Stack and then glue two more pieces to each key as shown.

11 Repeat step 10 for the rest of the keys, and leave to dry.

12 Tape the two sets of the **cardboard** Laptop and Laptop Side pieces together, forming two slim box forms as shown.

13 Sew the edges of each key together.

14 Sew the Laptop Screen to the Screen Border as shown.

15 Sew the Keypad Base to the Keyboard as shown.

16 Sew the Laptop Sides to the Laptop Top and Screen Border, leaving one side open.

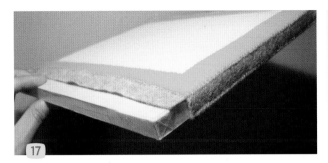

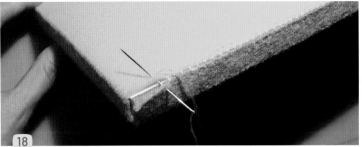

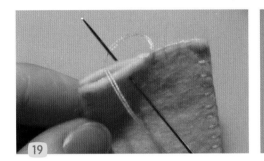

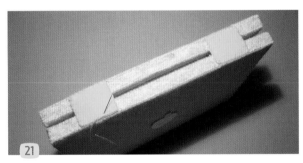

17 Insert one of the **cardboard** forms inside.

18 Sew the opening closed. Repeat steps 16 and 17 for the bottom half of the laptop.

19 Sew two pieces of the Laptop Hinges together with a blanket stitch. Repeat the same for the other set.

20 Glue the keys to the Keyboard as shown.

21 Sew the Laptop Hinges onto the laptop as shown.

22 Glue on the Scroll Pad and the Left and Right Select Keys. Sew the Side Supports to the sides of the laptop. Fold the Side Supports inwards to close your laptop. Sew the Pear Logo onto the top of the laptop.

MOUSE

    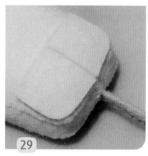

23 Sew the Mouse Side to the Mouse Top and Base, leaving an opening for stuffing.

24 Insert the **cardboard** Mouse piece into the base of the mouse as shown.

25 Fill the mouse with stuffing.

26 Stitch up the opening.

27 Glue the left and right Mouse Buttons onto the mouse.

28 Fold the Wire in half and sew the sides together as shown.

29 Sew one side of the wire to the mouse and the other side to the laptop.

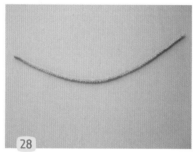  

SCREEN ICONS

30 Glue the Internet Icon together as shown.

31 Stitch the Trash Bin Icon and glue it onto the Trash Bin as shown.

32 Stitch the details on the Email Icon as shown.

33 Cut out the Messenger, Home, and Arrow Cursor. Glue the icons to the laptop screen as desired.

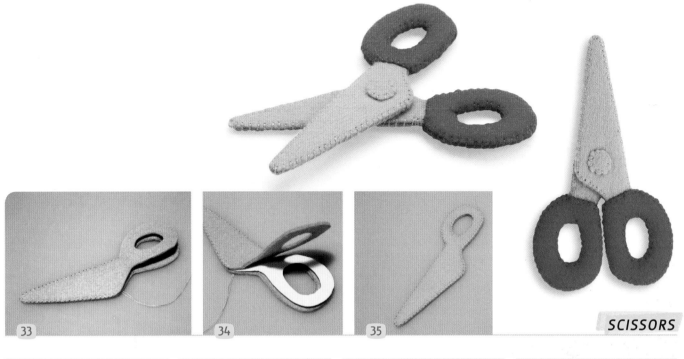

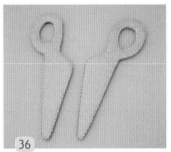

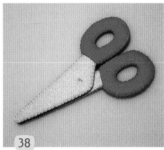

SCISSORS

33 Sew two felt Scissors pieces together, leaving the top open.

34 Insert one of the **cardboard** Scissors pieces as shown.

35 Stitch up the opening.

36 Repeat steps 33 through 35 for the other side.

37 Sew the Handles onto the Scissors.

38 Assemble the Scissors and stitch them together as shown.

39 Sew the Screw onto both sides, covering the stitches.

STAPLER

40

41

42

43

44

45

46

47

40 Sew the Top, Base, and Front of Stapler Parts A and B together.

41 Fold and tape the **cardboard** Stapler Parts A and B as shown.

42 Insert the cardboard forms into the Stapler Part A and B as shown.

43 Sew on the Stapler Part A and B Back pieces of the stapler.

44 Sew all the Stapler Center pieces together, leaving the front open and filling it with stuffing.

45 Stitch the opening closed.

46 Sew the Center to Stapler Part A as shown.

47 Stitch Part A and B together as shown.

GOLDEN YELLOW
10" x 13¾" (25cm x 35cm),
2 pieces

WHITE
15¾" x 15¾" (40cm x 40cm)

FADED GRAY
9" x 10" (23cm x 25cm)

DARK GRAY
1½" x 3½" (4cm x 9cm)

CHESTNUT BROWN
7" x 8¾" (18cm x 22cm)

COCOA BROWN
¾" x 1¼" (2cm x 3cm)

LEMON FROST
1½" x 3¼" (4cm x 8cm)

BABY PINK
¾" x ¾" (2cm x 2cm)

SKIN
1¼" x 3½" (3cm x 9cm)

BLUE
4" x 4¾ (10cm x 12cm)

GRAY
4" x 8" (10cm x 20cm)

CHILI RED
3¼" x 4" (8cm x 10cm)

BLACK
¾" x ¾" (2cm x 2cm)

BRIGHT YELLOW
8" x 8" (20cm x 20cm)

LIGHT GREEN
3¼" x 3¼" (8cm x 8cm)

SOFT BLUE
½" x ½" (1cm x 1cm)

GREEN
¾" x ¾" (2cm x 2cm)

BEIGE
1¼" x ¾" (3cm x 2cm)

ORANGE
¾" x ¾" (2cm x 2cm)

1mm-thick cardboard
23¼" x 16½" (59cm x 42cm),
4 pieces

Cellophane tape

Folding Line

FRONT & BACK
Chestnut Brown x 2
Cardboard x 2

SIDES
Chestnut Brown x 2
Cardboard x 2

SOLAR PANEL
Cocoa Brown x 1

TOP & BASE
Chestnut Brown x 2
Cardboard x 2

KEYPAD NUMBERS & SIGNS
White x 12
Lemon Frost x 5
Baby Pink x 1

NUMBER SCREEN BORDER
Skin x 1

KEYPAD ('+' SIGN)
Lemon Frost x 1

NUMBERS SCREEN
Dark Gray x 1

✳ Cut out according to measurements stated

✳ **LAPTOP TOP, BASE & KEYBOARD**
Golden Yellow x 3
6¾" x 9"
(17cm x 23cm)

✳ **LAPTOP SCREEN BORDER**
Golden Yellow x 1
6¾" x 9"
(17cm x 23cm),
¾" wide (2cm wide)

✳ **LAPTOP SCREEN**
White x 1
6¾" x 8¾" (16cm x 22cm)

✳ **KEYPAD BASE**
Faded Gray x 1
8¼" x 3½" (21cm x 9cm)

✳ **LAPTOP SIDES**
Faded Gray x 4
9" x ½" (23cm x 1.3cm)

✳ **LAPTOP SIDES**
Faded Gray x 4
6¾" x ½" (17cm x 1.3cm)

OFFICE

* Cut out according to measurements stated

LETTERS & NUMBERS KEY
White x 103

'ENTER' KEY
White x 3

LAPTOP SCROLL PAD
White x 1

LETTERS & NUMBERS KEY SIDES
White x 36

✱ LAPTOP (SIDES)
Cardboard x 4
6½" x ⁷⁄₁₆" (16.7cm x 1cm)

'ENTER' KEY SIDE
White x 1

✱ LAPTOP
Cardboard x 4
6½" x 8¾"
(16cm x 22cm)

SIDE SUPPORT
Faded Gray x 2

LEFT & RIGHT SELECT KEY
Dark Gray x 1

✱ LAPTOP (SIDES)
Cardboard x 4
11" x ⁷⁄₁₆" (22.7cm x 1cm)

LAPTOP HINGES
Golden Yellow x 4

A B C D E F G H I J K L M N
O P Q R S T U V W X Y Z
0 1 2 3 4 5 6 7 8 9

LETTERS & NUMBERS FOR KEYPAD

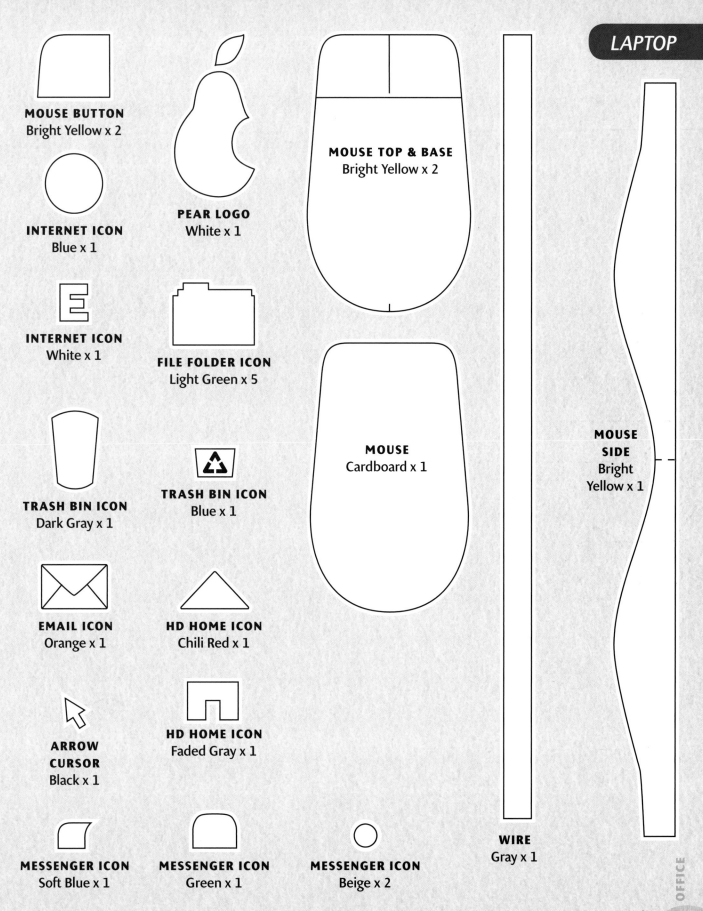

MOUSE BUTTON
Bright Yellow x 2

INTERNET ICON
Blue x 1

INTERNET ICON
White x 1

TRASH BIN ICON
Dark Gray x 1

EMAIL ICON
Orange x 1

ARROW CURSOR
Black x 1

MESSENGER ICON
Soft Blue x 1

PEAR LOGO
White x 1

FILE FOLDER ICON
Light Green x 5

TRASH BIN ICON
Blue x 1

HD HOME ICON
Chili Red x 1

HD HOME ICON
Faded Gray x 1

MESSENGER ICON
Green x 1

MESSENGER ICON
Beige x 2

MOUSE TOP & BASE
Bright Yellow x 2

MOUSE
Cardboard x 1

WIRE
Gray x 1

MOUSE SIDE
Bright Yellow x 1

OFFICE

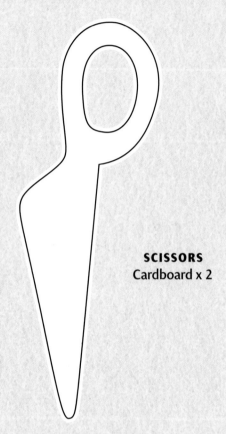

SCISSORS
Cardboard x 2

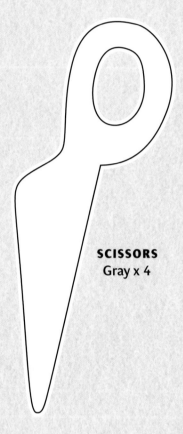

SCISSORS
Gray x 4

HANDLES
Chili Red x 4

SCREW
Gray x 2

STAPLER (PART A) TOP
Blue x 1

STAPLER (PART A) BASE
Blue x 1

STAPLER (PART B) BASE
Blue x 1

STAPLER (PART B) TOP
Blue x 1

STAPLER CENTER TOP & BASE
Gray x 2

STAPLER CENTER SIDES
Gray x 2

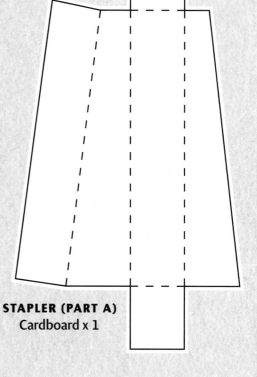

STAPLER (PART A)
Cardboard x 1

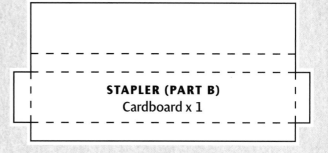

STAPLER (PART B)
Cardboard x 1

**STAPLER (PART A)
(FRONT)**
Blue x 1

**STAPLER (PART A)
(BACK)**
Blue x 1

**STAPLER (PART B)
(FRONT & BACK)**
Blue x 2

**STAPLER CENTER
FRONT**
Gray x 1

OFFICE

PLANTS

Happy plants forever. Watering? Never!

1 Stitch the details on all of the Big and Small Leaves.

2 Roll up the base of each leaf and sew it together as shown.

3 Snip the top of each Anther, then roll and sew it together.

4 Roll the Flower Stalks over the Anthers, and sew them together.

5 Slip the Flower Petal over the Stalk and Anther as shown, and stitch to secure. Repeat the same process for the other four Flowers.

6 Tie all the Flowers together as shown.

7 Arrange the Small Leaves around the Flowers, and tie them together.

8 Place the Big Leaves around the Small Leaves, and tie them together.

9 Stack the Inner and Outer Pot Sides, and sew them to the two stacked Pot Base pieces. Neaten the edge with a blanket stitch.

10 Cut an "X" on the Soil Top, and sew the Soil Top and Soil Side together.

11 Turn the pot over and place the **cardboard** Soil Top inside.

12 Insert the plant through the "X" in the Soil Top. Fill the Soil with stuffing, and sew the Soil Base on. Place the Soil into the Pot.

13

14

15

16

17

18

19

20

21

13 Sew two felt Cactus Sides together, and continue until you have 10 sets. Stitch all the sides together as shown.

14 Fill each Cactus Side with a thin layer of stuffing, then stuff the barrel of the cactus.

15 Sew the side of the Cactus Center together.

16 Place the Cactus Center in the middle of the Cactus as shown.

17 Sew the last two sides of the Cactus together

18 Sew the Cactus Center to the Cactus (on both ends) to secure it.

19 Stitch a Cactus Center End to one side of the Cactus as shown.

20 Turn the Cactus upside down and fill the Cactus Center with stuffing.

21 Stitch the second Cactus Center End over the opening to seal it.

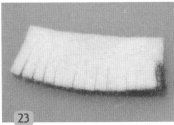

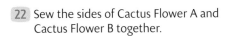

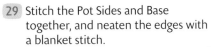

22 Sew the sides of Cactus Flower A and Cactus Flower B together.

23 Use a red marker and paint the tip of the Cactus Flower Filament as shown. Cut short slits where indicated on the pattern.

24 Roll the filament up and sew the sides together.

25 Stack the Cactus Flowers together with the Filament in the middle, and sew them together to secure.

26 Sew the Soil Sides and Soil Base together.

27 Fill the Soil with stuffing and sew the Soil Top on.

28 Sew the Flower on top of the Cactus, and the Cactus on top of the Soil as shown.

29 Stitch the Pot Sides and Base together, and neaten the edges with a blanket stitch.

30 Insert the Soil into the Pot.

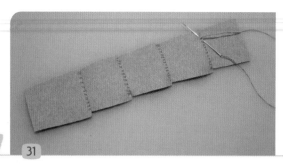

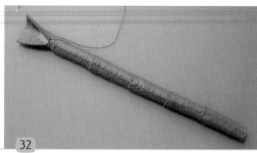

31

32

33

34

35

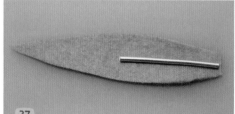

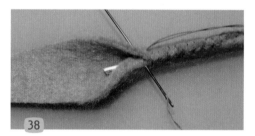

36

37

38

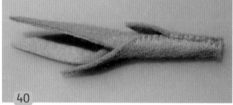

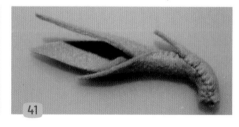

39

40

41

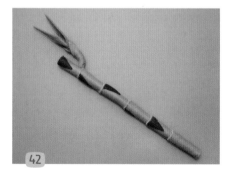

42

31 Sew six Bamboo Stem pieces together, overlapping each stem at the line indicated on the pattern.

32 Fold the stem in half and sew the sides together, filling it with stuffing as you sew.

33 Sew the Bamboo Top to the top of the Bamboo.

34 Stitch the Stem Design on the Bamboo as shown.

35 Glue the Bamboo Ring gently onto the Bamboo as shown.

36 Repeat steps 31 through 35 for the other two Bamboo.

37 Place a 1½'' (3.8 cm) long Aluminium Wire at the bottom center of the Large Leaf.

38 Roll up the end of the leaf and sew it together up to the line indicated on the pattern.

39 Sew another Large Leaf to the first leaf.

46 Turn the Soil over and insert the **cardboard** Soil Top as shown.

47 Insert the three Bamboo stalks through the "X's" into the Soil, making sure that the cardboard stays at the top.

48 Fill the Soil three-quarters of the way full with stuffing

49 Insert the **cardboard** Soil Base on top of the stuffing as shown.

50 Fill up the rest of the Soil with stuffing and sew the Soil Base on. Insert the Soil into the Pot.

40 Stitch on a Medium Leaf followed by a Small Leaf.

41 Bend the end of the leaf slightly to a 90° angle.

42 Sew the leaf to the Bamboo as shown. Repeat steps 37 through 42 to make the other two Bamboo stalks.

43 Sew the side of the Inner and Outer Pot pieces together, then neaten the top edge with a blanket stitch.

44 Sew the Pot Base to the Pot.

45 Cut 3 "X"s on the Soil Top, and then sew the Soil Top and Soil Side together as shown.

GREEN
12 x 8" (30cm x 20cm)

DARK PURPLE
8" x 6" (20cm x 15cm)

BRIGHT YELLOW
¾" x 1½" (2cm x 4cm)

CHESTNUT BROWN
8¾" x 10¼" (22cm x 26cm)

COCOA
6" x 9½" (15cm x 24cm)

CANDY PINK
5½" x 15¾" (14cm x 40cm)

WALNUT BROWN
6" x 8¼" (15cm x 21cm)
7" x 9½" (18cm x 24cm)

DARK GREEN
6¼" x 12" (16cm x 30cm)
4" x 4" (10cm x 10cm)

YELLOW
2" x 2½" (5cm x 6cm)

LEMON FROST
2 x 2½" (5cm x 6cm)

WHITE
¾" x 1½" (2cm x 4cm)

LEAF GREEN
8" x 15¾" (20cm x 40cm)

TUNA
2½" x 4" (6cm x 10cm)

FADED GREY
10¼" x 10¼" (26cm x 26cm)

1mm-thick cardboard
3¼" x 3¼" (8cm x 8cm)
7" x 4" (18cm x 10cm)

Red Marker Pen

Aluminum wire
(2mm thick x 12cm)

Wire cutters

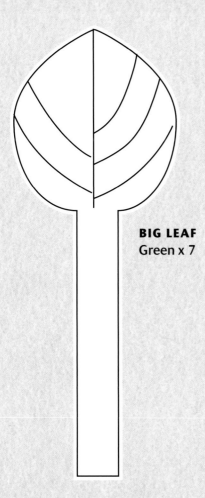

BIG LEAF
Green x 7

SMALL LEAF
Green x 6

FLOWER PETALS
Dark Purple x 5

FLOWER ANTHERS
Bright Yellow x 5

FLOWER STALK
Dark Purple x 5

SOIL TOP
Cardboard x 1

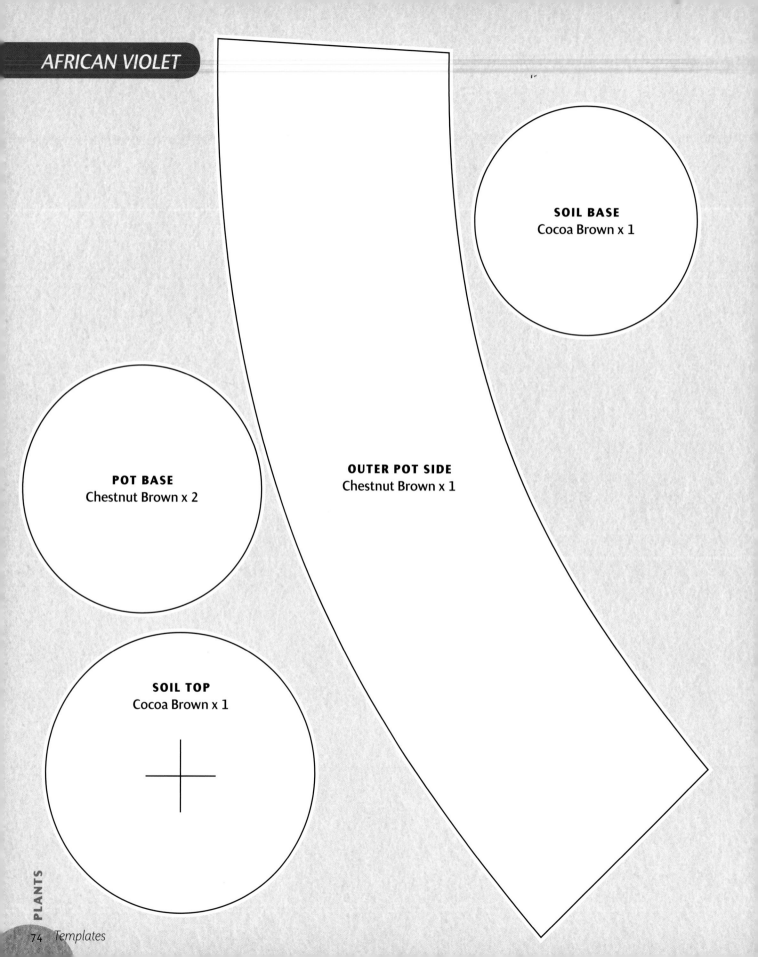

SOIL BASE
Cocoa Brown x 1

POT BASE
Chestnut Brown x 2

OUTER POT SIDE
Chestnut Brown x 1

SOIL TOP
Cocoa Brown x 1

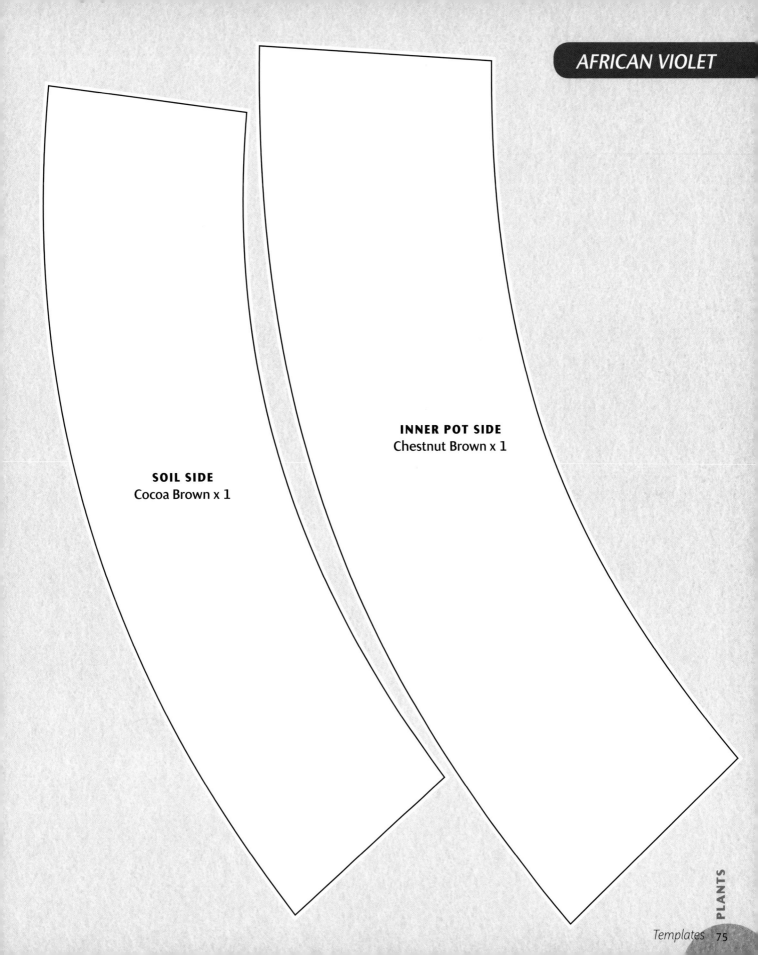

SOIL SIDE
Cocoa Brown x 1

INNER POT SIDE
Chestnut Brown x 1

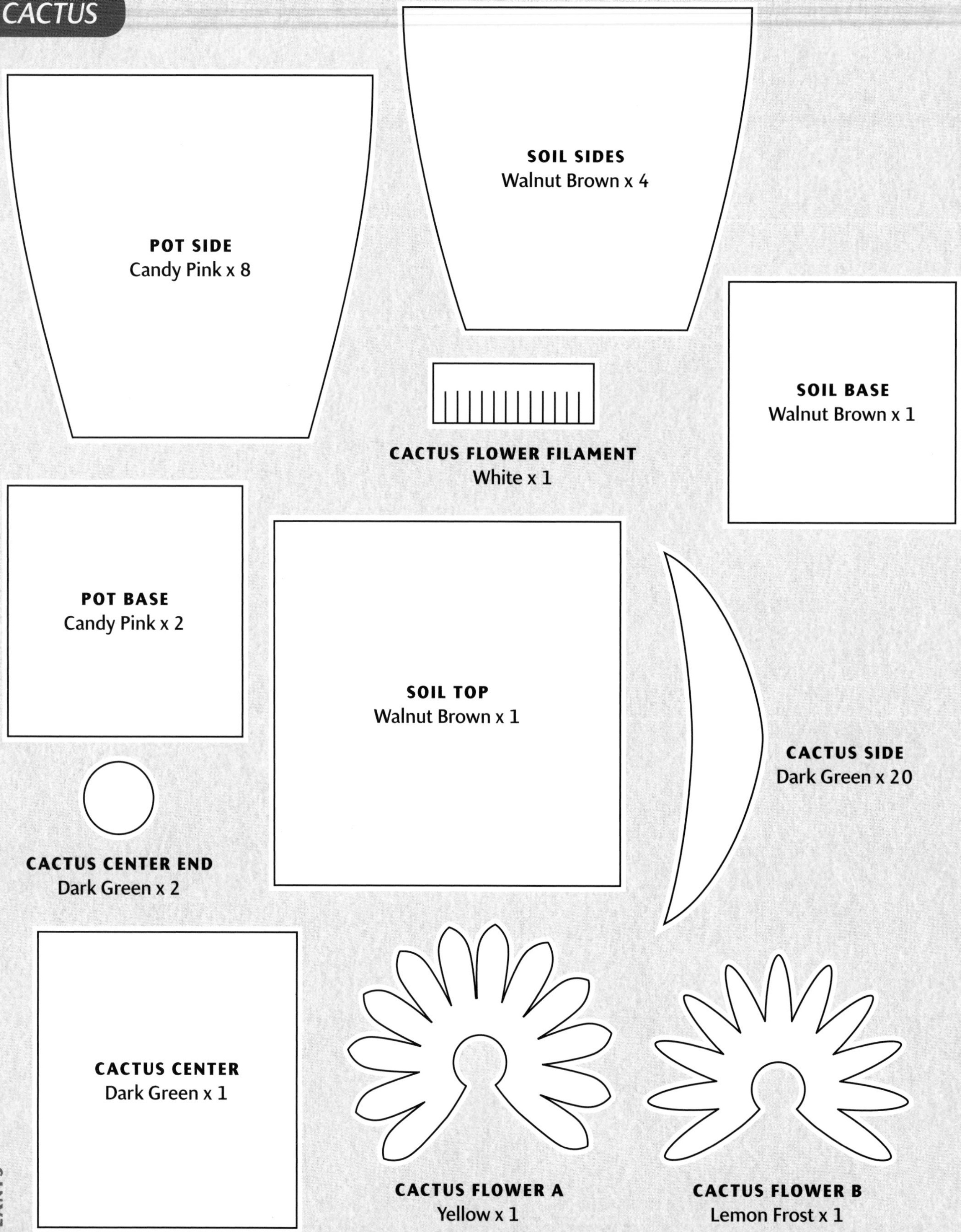

POT SIDE
Candy Pink x 8

SOIL SIDES
Walnut Brown x 4

SOIL BASE
Walnut Brown x 1

CACTUS FLOWER FILAMENT
White x 1

POT BASE
Candy Pink x 2

SOIL TOP
Walnut Brown x 1

CACTUS SIDE
Dark Green x 20

CACTUS CENTER END
Dark Green x 2

CACTUS CENTER
Dark Green x 1

CACTUS FLOWER A
Yellow x 1

CACTUS FLOWER B
Lemon Frost x 1

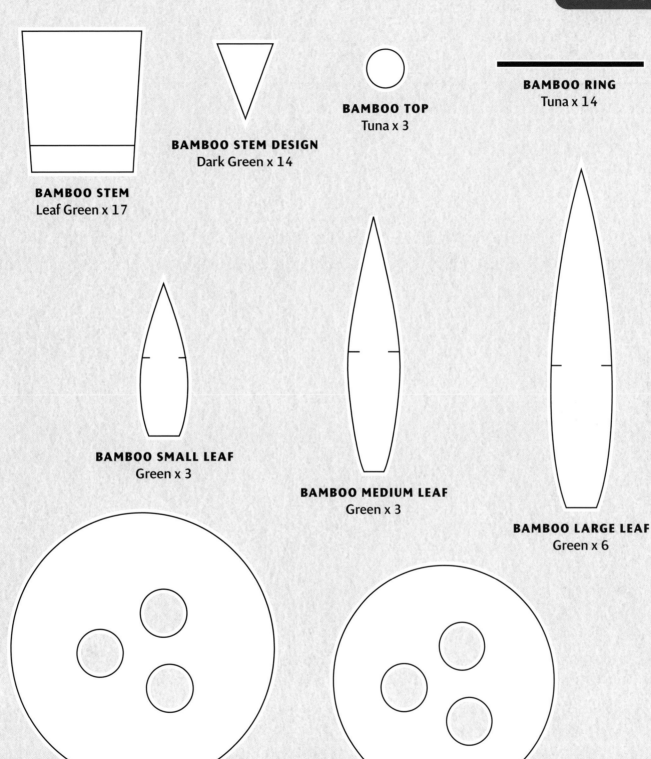

BAMBOO STEM
Leaf Green x 17

BAMBOO STEM DESIGN
Dark Green x 14

BAMBOO TOP
Tuna x 3

BAMBOO RING
Tuna x 14

BAMBOO SMALL LEAF
Green x 3

BAMBOO MEDIUM LEAF
Green x 3

BAMBOO LARGE LEAF
Green x 6

SOIL TOP
Cardboard x 1

SOIL BASE
Cardboard x 1

PLANTS

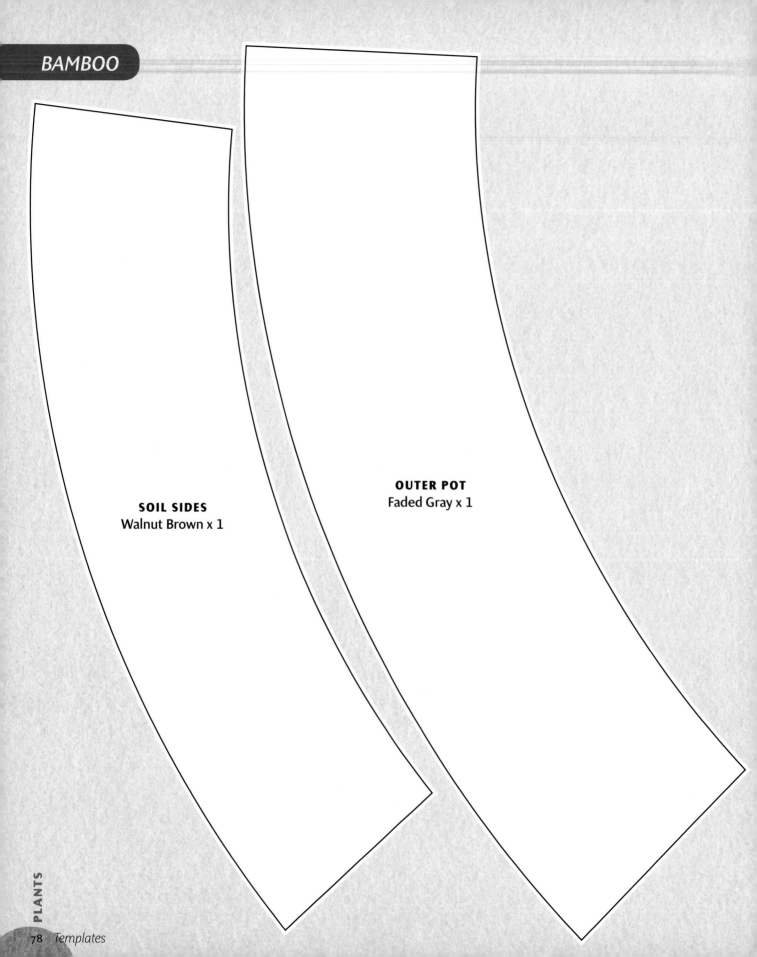

SOIL SIDES
Walnut Brown x 1

OUTER POT
Faded Gray x 1

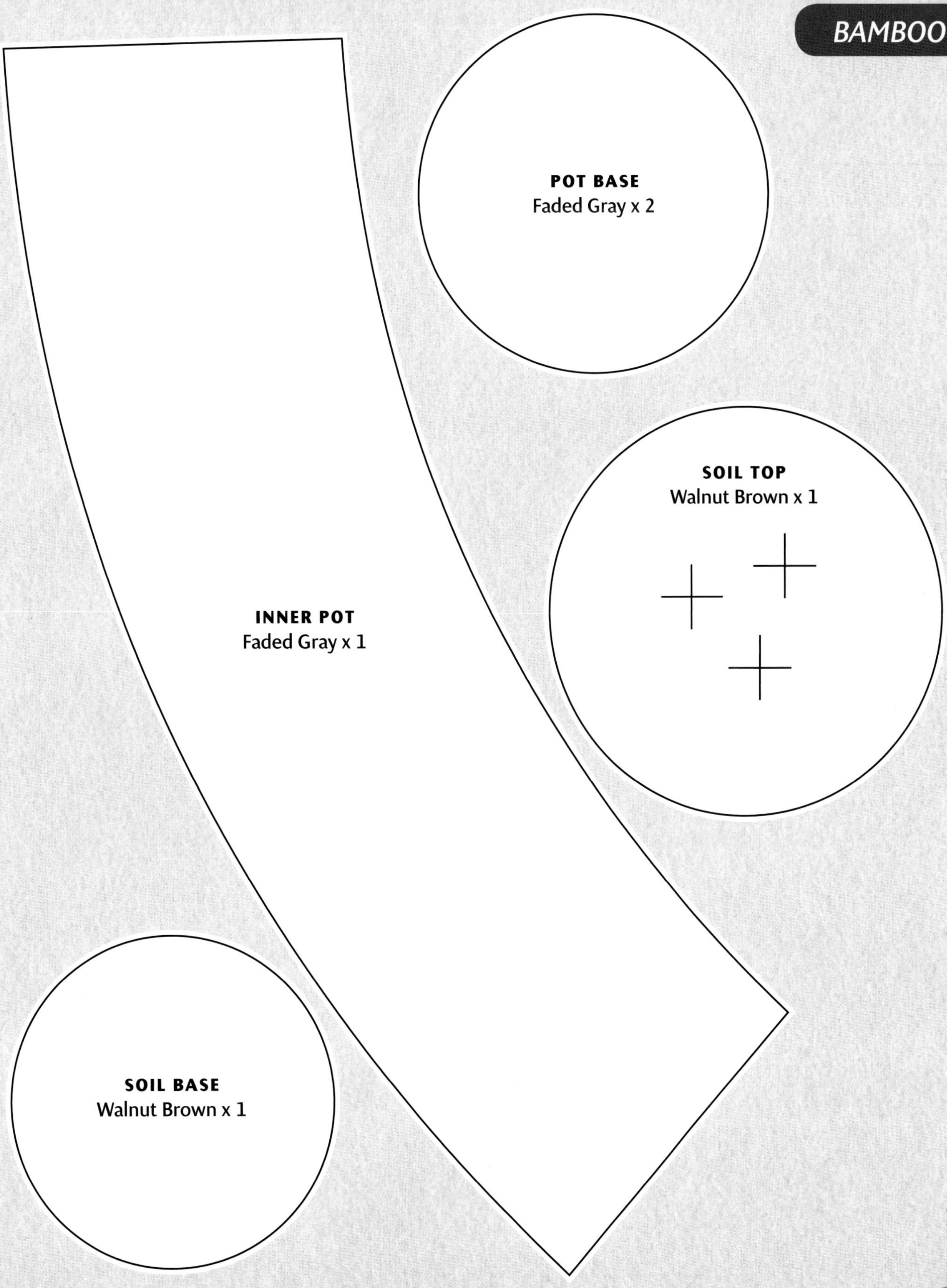

POT BASE
Faded Gray x 2

SOIL TOP
Walnut Brown x 1

INNER POT
Faded Gray x 1

SOIL BASE
Walnut Brown x 1

HOLIDAY

Holiday cheer for anytime of year.

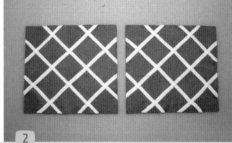

GINGERBREAD HOUSE

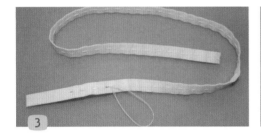

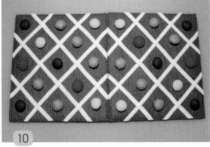

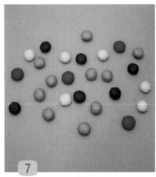

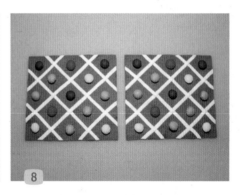

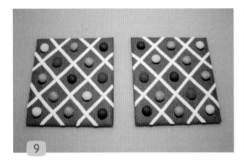

1. Cut the Criss Cross Roof Top Felt Ribbon into half as shown.

2. Sew the Felt Ribbon onto the Roof Tops as shown.

3. Stitch a running stitch about 5mm evenly down the center of the Roof Snow Borders as shown.

4. Pull the thread at one end until the ribbon gathers to about 5" (12.5cm) long. Knot the thread end, and trim off the excess thread.

5. Next, turn the ribbon in a closewise direction so it looks like the photo.

6. Repeat steps 3 through 5 with the remaining five strips.

7. Sew all the Chocolate Candies together, filling them with stuffing.

8. Sew all the Chocolate Candies onto the Roof as shown.

9. Sew the Roof Bases to the Roof Tops, inserting the **cardboard** Roofs in between.

10. Sew the Roofs together as shown.

11. Glue the Roof Snow Borders around the Roof as shown.

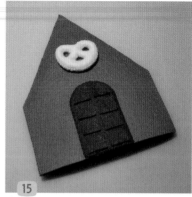

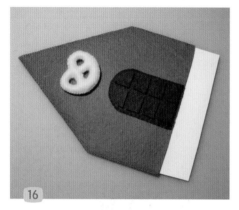

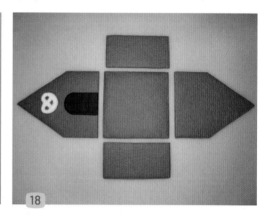

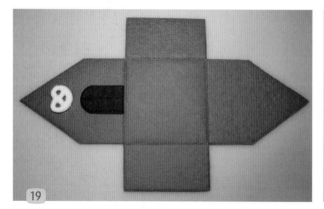

12 Sew the Pretzel together, filling it with stuffing as you sew.

13 Glue the Door Panels to the Gingerbread House Door.

14 Sew the Pretzel and the Door onto the Gingerbread House Front.

15 Sew a second Front piece to the Gingerbread House Front, leaving the bottom open as shown.

16 Insert the **cardboard** Front.

17 Stitch up the opening.

18 Repeat steps 15 through 17 for the Sides, Back, and Base of the Gingerbread House.

19 Sew the Front, Sides, and Back to the Base of the Gingerbread House as shown.

20 Stitch all the sides together.

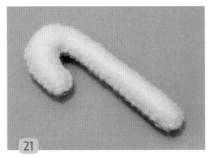

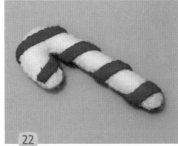

21 Sew two pieces of the Candy Cane together, filling it with stuffing as you go.

22 Twirl the Candy Cane Stripe around the Candy Cane, and sew together.

23 Do the same for the other cane.

24 Glue the Candy Canes to the Front of the house as shown.

25 Place the Roof on the House.

COOKIES

26 Sew the Snowman Cookie Front, Back, and Side together, filling it with a thin layer of stuffing.

27 Repeat the same for all the other cookies.

28 Stitch the details onto the Icing for the Christmas Tree, Snowman, and Candy Cookies.

29 Sew all the Icings onto the respective Cookies as shown.

30 Sew a gold string of about 4'' (10cm) long to the top of each cookie, and knot the ends.

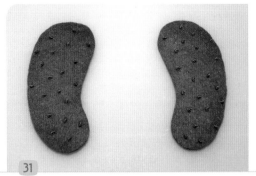

PICKLE ORNAMENT

31 Stitch French knots on each side of the Pickle Ornament.

32 Sew the Pickle together, filling it with stuffing.

33 Sew the Pickle Stem Top, Base, and Side together, filling with stuffing.

34 Sew the Stem onto the top of the Pickle.

35 Sew gold string onto the stem.

MILK GLASS

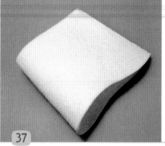

36 Using nylon thread, sew the **plastic** Milk Glass Side and Milk Glass Base together.

37 Stitch the Milk Side together.

38 Stitch on the Milk Top.

39 Fill the Milk with stuffing and sew the Milk Base on.

40 Place the Milk inside the Glass.

GINGERBREAD & NOTE

41 Glue the details onto the Gingerbread Boy and Girl as shown.

42 Sew the Sides and the Back on, and fill with stuffing.

43 Glue the Letters onto the Note.

CHESTNUT BROWN
15¾" x 15¾" (40cm x 40cm),
2 pieces

WHITE
12" x 12" (30cm x 30cm)

GINGERBREAD
4" x 12" (10cm x 30cm)

GREEN
2¾" x 2¾" (7cm x 7cm)

CHILI RED
4" x 8" (10cm x 20cm)

IVORY
2½" x 3¼" (6cm x 8cm)

MADELEINE
12" x 15¾" (30cm x 40cm)

PINK
1¼" x 2" (3cm x 5cm)

LIGHT PURPLE
1¼" x 2" (3cm x 5cm)

LIGHT GREEN
1½" x 1½" (4cm x 4cm)

BRIGHT YELLOW
1½" x 4" (4cm x 10cm)

COCOA BROWN
2¾" x 3½" (7cm x 9cm)

DARK GREEN
4" x 4" (10cm x 10cm)

LEMON FROST
1¼" x 1½" (3cm x 4cm)

BLUE
2½" x 3¼" (6cm x 8cm)

LEAF GREEN
2½" x 3¼" (6cm x 8cm)

ORANGE
2½" x 3¼" (6cm x 8cm)

1mm-thick cardboard
23¼" x 16½" (59cm x 42cm),
2 pieces

Ivory Felt ribbon
⁷⁄₁₆" x 15' 6" (1cm x 472cm)

Non-toxic craft glue

PVC plastic sheet
8" x 9½" (20cm x 24cm)

Nylon thread/fishing line
5' (150cm)

Gold String

✳ Cut out according to measurements stated

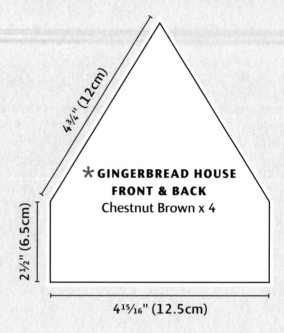

✳ **GINGERBREAD HOUSE BASE**
Chestnut Brown x 2
4¹⁵/₁₆" x 4¹⁵/₁₆"
(12.5cm x 12.5cm)

✳ **GINGERBREAD HOUSE FRONT & BACK**
Chestnut Brown x 4

4¾" (12cm)

2½" (6.5cm)

4¹⁵/₁₆" (12.5cm)

✳ **GINGERBREAD HOUSE SIDES**
Chestnut Brown x 4
4¹⁵/₁₆" x 2½" (12.5cm x 6.5cm)

✳ **GINGERBREAD HOUSE ROOF TOP & BASE**
Chestnut Brown x 4
5¾" x 5⅛" (14.5cm x 13cm)

CRISS CROSS ROOF TOP
Ivory Felt Ribbon – 50 cm x 1 Strip
19¾" (50cm)

ROOF SNOW BORDERS
Ivory Felt Ribbon – 120 cm x 2 Strips – 60cm x 3 Strips
47¼" (120cm) x 2 strips
23⅝" (60cm) x 3 strips

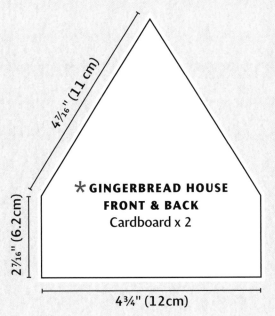

∗ GINGERBREAD HOUSE FRONT & BACK
Cardboard x 2

4⁷⁄₁₆" (11 cm)

2⁷⁄₁₆" (6.2cm)

4¾" (12cm)

∗ GINGERBREAD HOUSE SIDES
Cardboard x 2
4¾" x 2⅜" (12cm x 6cm)

∗ GINGERBREAD HOUSE ROOF
Cardboard x 2
5½" x 4¹³⁄₁₆" (14cm x 12.3cm)

∗ GINGERBREAD HOUSE BASE
Cardboard x 1
4¾" x 4¾" (12cm x 12cm)

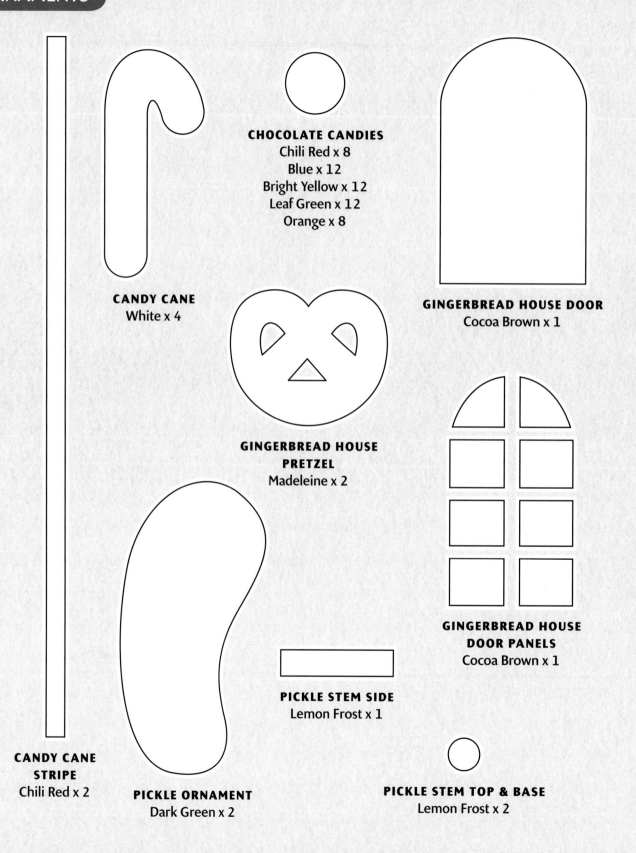

CANDY CANE
White x 4

CHOCOLATE CANDIES
Chili Red x 8
Blue x 12
Bright Yellow x 12
Leaf Green x 12
Orange x 8

GINGERBREAD HOUSE DOOR
Cocoa Brown x 1

GINGERBREAD HOUSE PRETZEL
Madeleine x 2

GINGERBREAD HOUSE DOOR PANELS
Cocoa Brown x 1

PICKLE STEM SIDE
Lemon Frost x 1

CANDY CANE STRIPE
Chili Red x 2

PICKLE ORNAMENT
Dark Green x 2

PICKLE STEM TOP & BASE
Lemon Frost x 2

**SNOWMAN COOKIE
FRONT & BACK**
Madeleine x 2

**SNOWMAN
COOKIE ICING**
White x 1

**SNOWMAN
BUTTONS**
Chestnut
Brown x 2

**CANDY COOKIES
FRONT & BACK**
Madeleine x 4

**CANDY COOKIES
ICING**
Pink x 1
Light Purple x 1

**SNOW FLAKE COOKIE
FRONT & BACK**
Madeleine x 2

**SNOW FLAKE
COOKIE ICING**
White x 1

**CHRISTMAS TREE COOKIE
FRONT & BACK**
Madeleine x 2

**CHRISTMAS TREE
COOKIE ICING**
Green x 1

**STAR COOKIES
FRONT & BACK**
Madeleine x 4

STAR COOKIES ICING
Light Green x 1
Bright Yellow x 1

**BOOT COOKIE
FRONT & BACK**
Madeleine x 2

BOOT COOKIE ICING
Chestnut Brown x 1

COOKIES SIDE
Madeleine x 8

HOLIDAY

MILK GLASS SIDE
PVC Plastic Sheet x 1

MILK GLASS BASE
PVC Plastic Sheet x 1

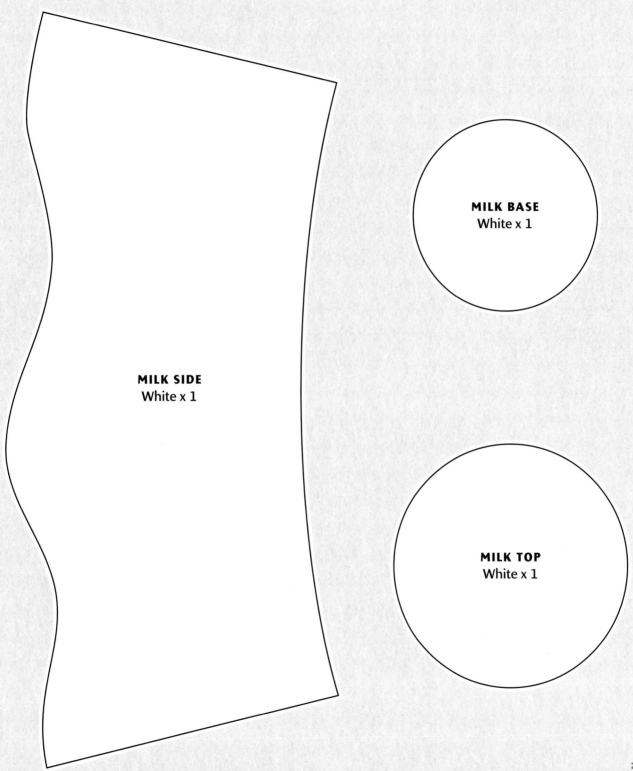

MILK BASE
White x 1

MILK SIDE
White x 1

MILK TOP
White x 1

GINGERBREAD BOY & GIRL

 Cut out according to measurements stated

RIBBON
Green x 1
Chili Red x 1

BUTTONS
Green x 2
Chili Red x 2

BORDERS
Ivory x 8

EYES
Ivory x 4

MOUTH
Ivory x 2

GINGERBREAD BOY & GIRL
Gingerbread x 4

* **GINGERBREAD BOY & GIRL SIDES**
Gingerbread x 2
12" x ⁵⁄₁₆" (30cm x .8cm)

For Santa

**FOR SANTA LETTERS
ON NOTE**
Chili Red x 1 each

NOTE
White x 1

VEGGIES

How does your garden grow?
With needle and thread and stitches in a row.

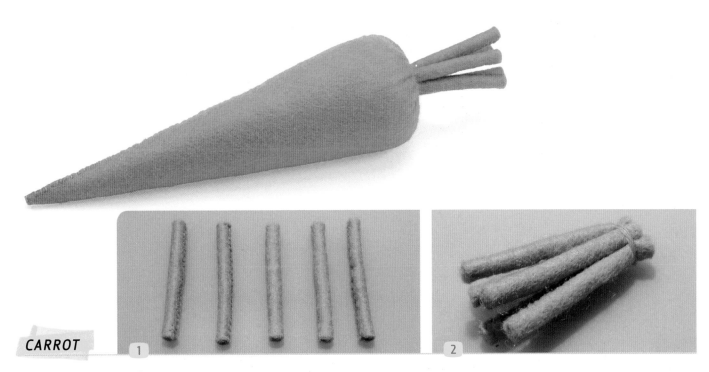

1. Roll up and sew the Carrot Leaves as shown.

2. Tie one end of the Carrot Leaves together as shown.

3. Sew the side of the Carrot together.

4. Sew a running stitch around the edge of the Carrot, leaving the thread ends loose.

5. Fill the Carrot with stuffing.

6. Pull both ends of the threads, leaving an opening just big enough to insert the leaves, and then fasten the threads with knots. Trim away any excess threads.

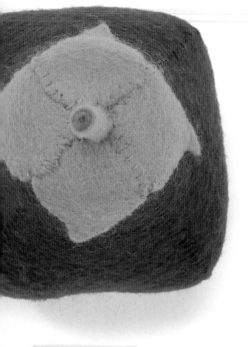

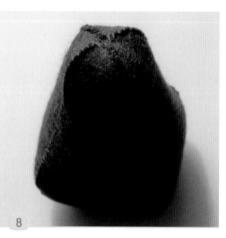

7

8

9

10

11

7 Sew the Eggplant Sides together and fill it with stuffing.

8 Stitch the opening closed.

9 Sew the Leaves on top of the Eggplant as shown.

10 Roll up and sew the longer side of the Eggplant Stem.

11 Sew the Stem on top of the Eggplant.

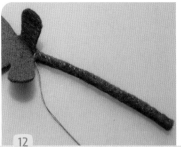

RED RADISH

12 Roll up the base of the Radish leaf and stitch it together as shown.

13 Fold the Leaf in half and stitch the vein detail down the center using a backstitch.

14 Stitch the rest of the vein details on the Leaf.

15 Repeat the same for two more Leaves.

16 Place them in a bunch and tie the ends together as shown.

17 Sew the Radish Sides together, leaving an opening for stuffing.

18 Fill with stuffing, leaving a small opening for the Leaves.

19 Insert the Leaves into the Radish and sew them together.

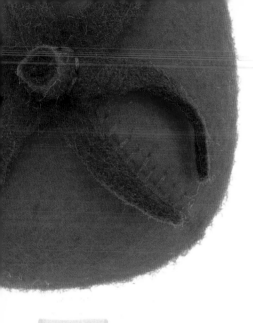

TOMATO

20 Sew the sides of the tomato together, leaving an opening for stuffing.

21 Fill the tomato with stuffing and seal up the opening.

22 Roll up the long side of the Tomato Stem and sew it together.

23 Sew the Tomato Leaves on top of the Tomato as shown.

24 Sew the Stem on top.

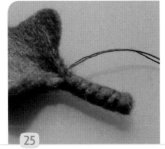

WHITE RADISH

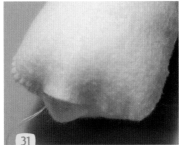

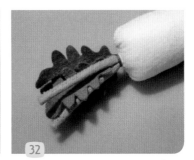

25 Roll up and then sew the base of the White Radish Leaf together as shown.

26 Fold the Leaf in half and stitch the center detail vein with a backstitch as shown.

27 Repeat the same process for the other two Leaves.

28 Roll up and then sew the three Leaf Stalks together as shown.

29 Put all the leaves and stalks in a bunch and tie the ends together.

30 Sew the two White Radish Sides together, leaving the top open.

31 Fill the radish with stuffing.

32 Insert the Leaves in the center and stitch up the opening.

ORANGE
6" x 6¾" (15cm x 17cm)

LEAF GREEN
3¼" x 4" (8cm x 10cm)

DARK GREEN
6" x 9½" (15cm x 24cm)

CHERRY RED
4" x 7" (10cm x 18cm)

CHILI RED
3½" x 6¼" (9cm x 16cm)

GREEN TEA
4" x 6" (10cm x 15cm)

DARK PURPLE
5" x 8" (13cm x 20cm)

DIRTY GREEN
3¼" x 6" (8cm x 15cm)

WHITE
5½" x 6" (14cm x 15cm)

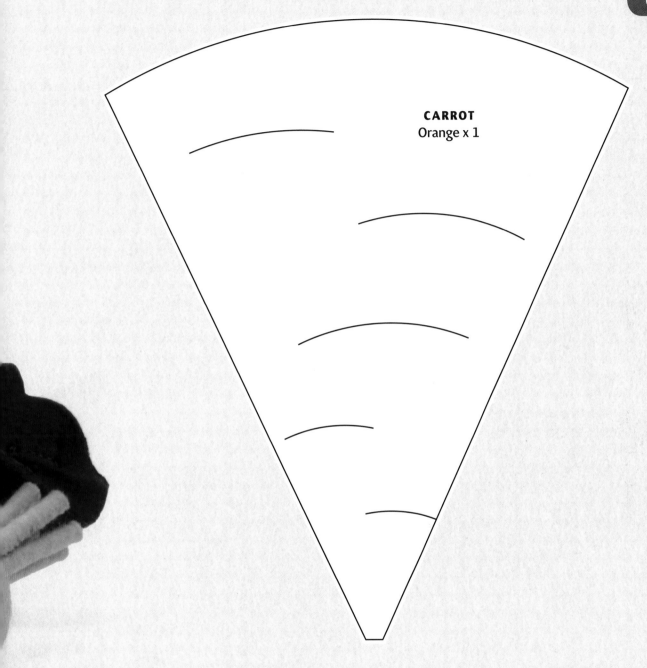

CARROT
Orange x 1

CARROT
Leaf Green x 5

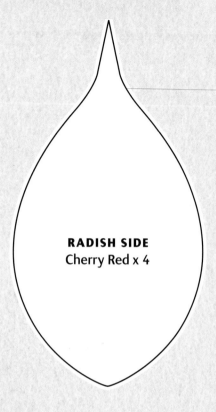

RADISH SIDE
Cherry Red x 4

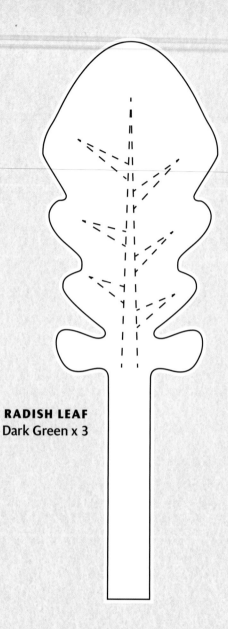

RADISH LEAF
Dark Green x 3

TOMATO SIDE
Chili Red x 4

TOMATO STEM
Dark Green x 1

TOMATO LEAVES
Dark Green x 1

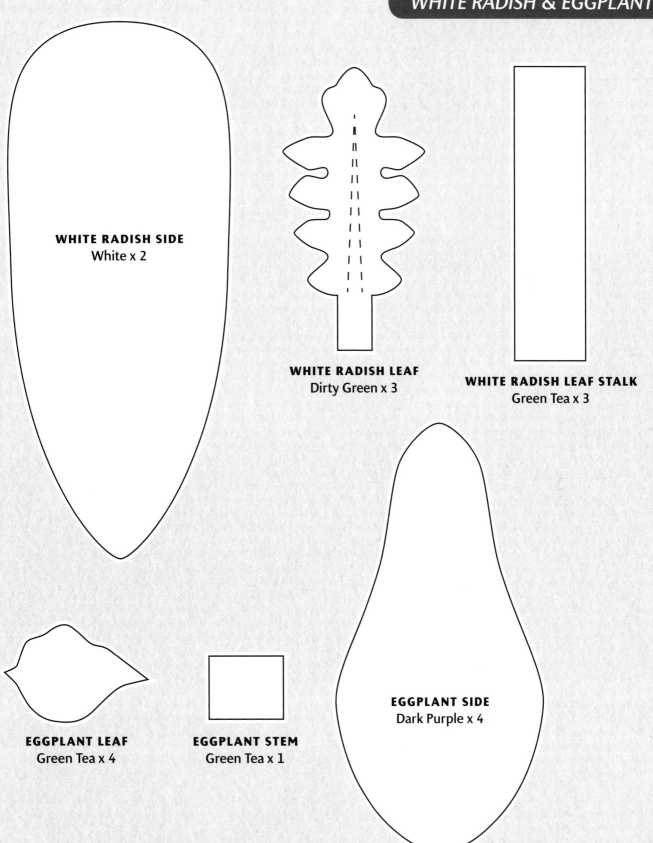

WHITE RADISH SIDE
White x 2

WHITE RADISH LEAF
Dirty Green x 3

WHITE RADISH LEAF STALK
Green Tea x 3

EGGPLANT LEAF
Green Tea x 4

EGGPLANT STEM
Green Tea x 1

EGGPLANT SIDE
Dark Purple x 4

DOCTOR

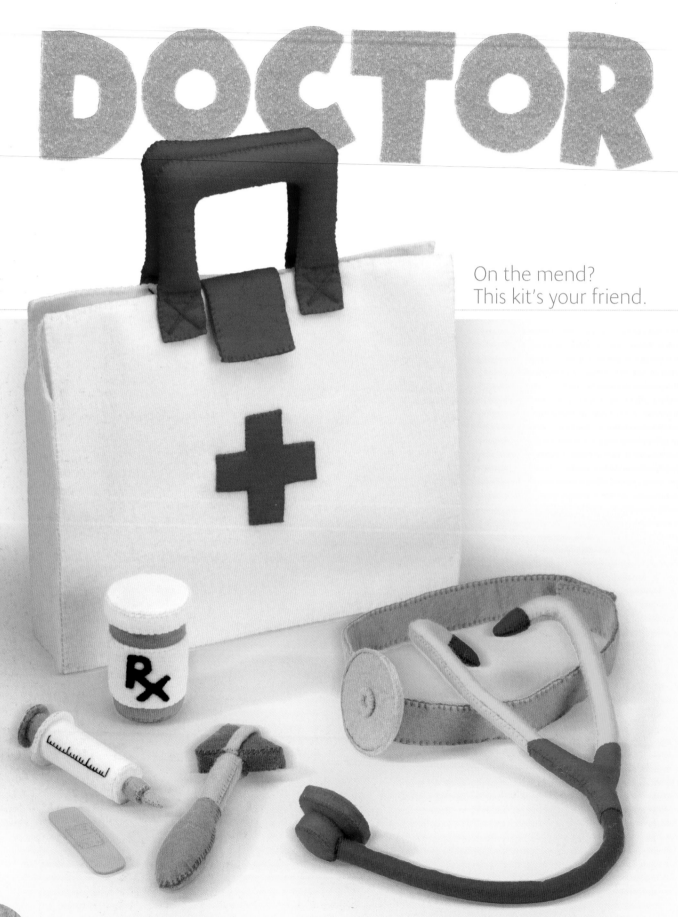

On the mend?
This kit's your friend.

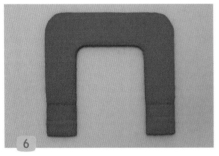

1 Sew the Logo onto the Front of the bag.

2 Sew the Front, Back, Sides, and Base of the bag together as shown.

3 Neaten the edges of the bag with a blanket stitch.

4 Sew the two Closure pieces together with a blanket stitch.

5 Sew the Closure onto the bag and then sew on the hook-and-loop Fasteners.

6 Sew the details and the inner part of the Handle together as shown.

7 Sew the outer part of the Handle together, filling it with stuffing as you sew.

8 Sew the Handles onto the bag, making an "X" with your stitching.

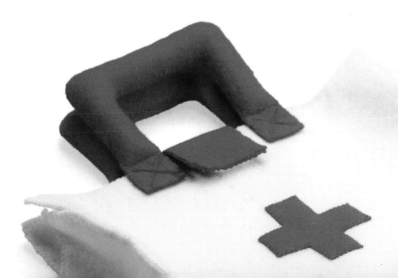

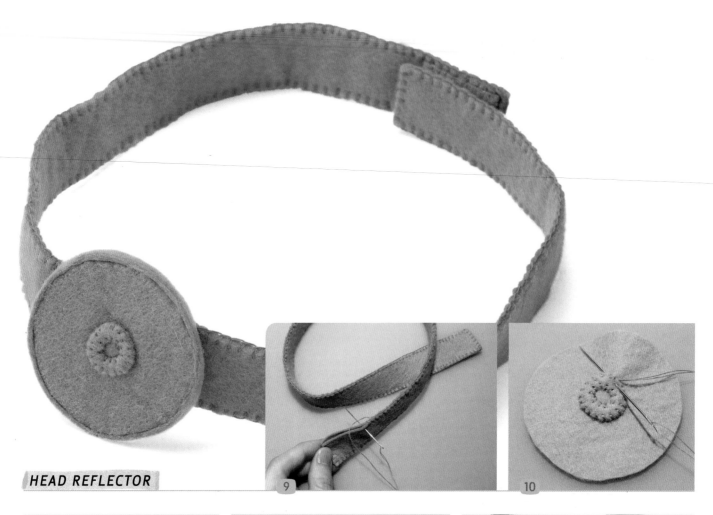

HEAD REFLECTOR

9 Sew the Head Bands together using a blanket stitch.

10 Sew the Reflector Center to one piece of the Reflector.

11 Place the two pieces of the Reflector together and apply glue to the edge as shown.

12 Glue the Reflector Bias around the light reflector. Trim off any excess fabric, and let the piece dry.

13 Sew the Fasteners onto the ends of the head band. Sew the light reflector onto the center of the head band.

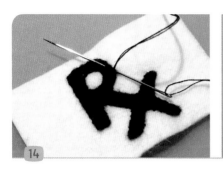

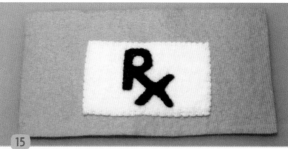

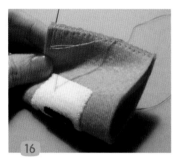

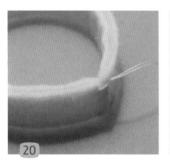

14 Sew the Wording onto the Label.

15 Sew the Label onto the Outside.

16 Stack the Bottle Inside and Outside pieces and sew the sides together.

17 Sew on the Bottle Base.

18 Fill the bottle with stuffing.

19 Sew on the Bottle Top.

20 Sew the Bottle Cap Outside and Inside pieces together.

21 Sew the Bottle Cap to the Sides as shown.

22 Turn the Cap over and neaten the edges with a blanket stitch. Place the cap on the bottle.

DOCTOR

Prescription Bottle 109

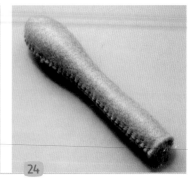

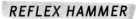

REFLEX HAMMER

`23`

`24`

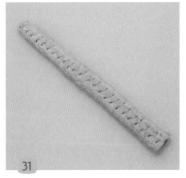

`25`

`26`

`27`

`28`

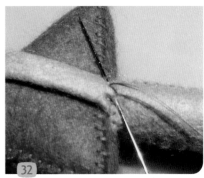

`29`

`30`

`31`

`32`

23 Sew the sides of the Handle together, leaving the top open for stuffing.

24 Fill the handle with stuffing.

25 Fold and then sew the Rubber Head together, leaving an opening for stuffing.

26 Fill the Rubber Head with stuffing and stitch up the opening.

27 Shape your rubber head into a neat triangle as shown.

28 Sew the Handle Grip to the handle.

29 Sew the rubber head onto the handle.

30 Sew the sides of the Rubber Head Support together.

31 Press the support down flat so the stitches are at the center.

32 Wrap the support around the rubber head and sew it on.

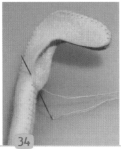

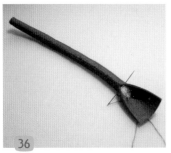

33 Sew the outer parts of the Ear Tube together.

34 Sew the inner parts of the Ear Tube together, stuffing as you sew.

35 Sew the Ear Pieces to the Ear Tube.

36 Sew the sides of the tubing together, filling it with stuffing as you sew.

37 Sew the tubing to the ear tube.

38 Sew the outer parts of the Stem together as shown.

39 Insert the Stem from the end of the Tubing as shown.

40 Sew the Stem to the Ear Tube.

41 Sew the Chest Piece Side to one of the Chest Pieces. Stitch the other Chest Piece on top, leaving an opening for stuffing.

42 Stuff the Chest Piece and sew the opening closed.

43 Repeat steps 41 and 42 for the Chest Piece Head.

44 Sew the Chest Piece Head to the Chest Piece as shown.

45 Sew the Chest Piece to the end of the Tubing.

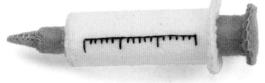

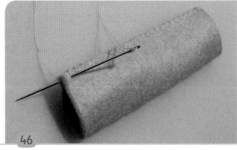

SYRINGE

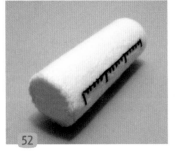

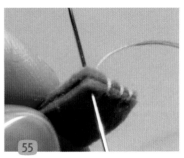

46 Sew the sides of the Plunger together.

47 Stitch the Plunger Top to the Plunger, filling with stuffing as you sew.

48 Sew the two Thumb Rest pieces together using a blanket stitch.

49 Sew the Thumb Rest to the Plunger.

50 Stitch the details onto the Barrel Outside.

51 Stack the Barrel Inside and the Barrel Outside pieces, and then sew the sides together.

52 Sew the Barrel Base to the Barrel.

53 Stitch the outside of the Finger Flange pieces together using a blanket stitch.

54 Sew the Finger Flange to the top of the Barrel.

55 Sew the sides of the Needle Hub Side together.

56

57

58

59

56 Sew the Needle Hub Top and Base to the Needle Hub Side as shown.

57 Sew the Needle Hub to the Base of the Barrel.

58 Stitch the sides of the needle together, leaving an opening for stuffing.

59 Fill the Needle with stuffing.

60 Sew the Needle to the Needle Hub. Insert the Plunger into the Barrel.

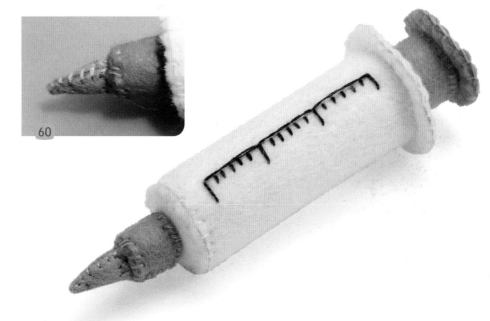

60

61

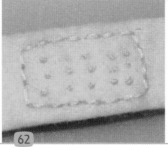

62

63

61 Stitch the details on the center of the bandage using a backstitch.

62 Sew a row of French knots onto the bandage as shown.

63 Turn the bandage over and glue the Bandage Center piece on as shown.

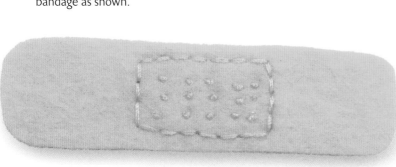

DOCTOR

Adhesive Bandage   **113**

WHITE
15¾" x 15¾" (40cm x 40cm)

CHILI RED
15¾" x 15¾" (40cm x 40cm)

YELLOW
6" x 12" (15cm x 30cm)

BLUE
2½" x 9" (6cm x 23cm)

PEACOCK BLUE
2½" x 6¼" (6cm x 16cm)

GRAY
4" x 9½" (10cm x 24cm)

ORANGE
5½" x 6¼" (14cm x 16cm)

BLACK
1½" x 1½" (4cm x 4cm)

SOFT BLUE
12" x 1¼" (30cm x 3cm), 3 pieces

WALNUT BROWN
5½" x 4" (14cm x 10cm)

PURPLE
2" x 3¼" (5cm x 8cm)

GOLDEN YELLOW
3¼" x 1¼" (8cm x 3cm)

White hook-and-loop fasteners
1¼" x 1¼" (3cm x 3cm), 2 sets

* Cut out according to measurements stated

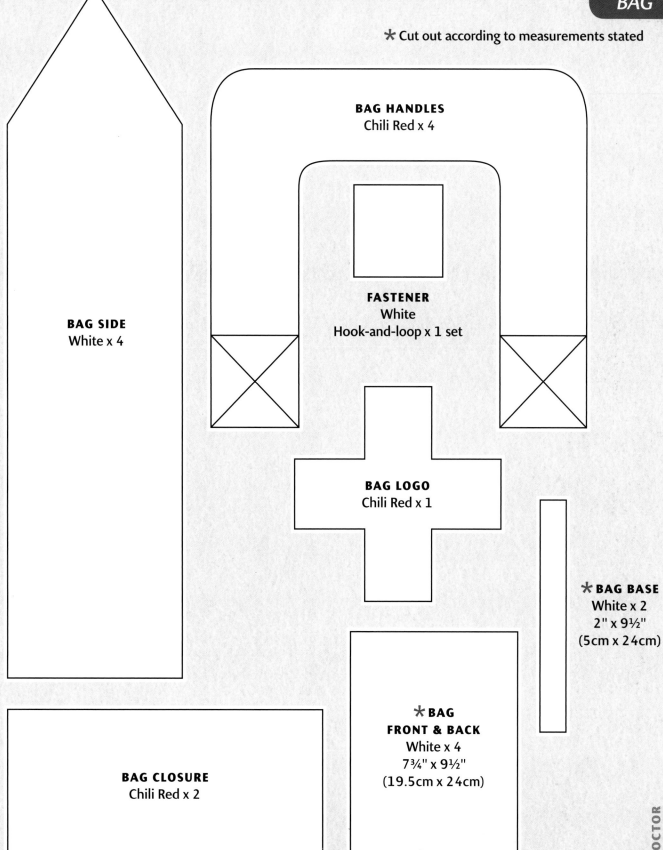

BAG HANDLES
Chili Red x 4

FASTENER
White
Hook-and-loop x 1 set

BAG SIDE
White x 4

BAG LOGO
Chili Red x 1

✳ BAG BASE
White x 2
2" x 9½"
(5cm x 24cm)

**✳ BAG
FRONT & BACK**
White x 4
7¾" x 9½"
(19.5cm x 24cm)

BAG CLOSURE
Chili Red x 2

HEAD REFLECTOR

✳ Cut out according to measurements stated

REFLECTOR
Gray x 2

REFLECTOR CENTER
Gray x 1

FASTENER
Hook-and-loop Fastener x 1 set

REFLECTOR BIAS
Gray x 1

✳ HEAD BAND
Soft Blue x 2
20¼" x 1" (52cm x 2.5cm)

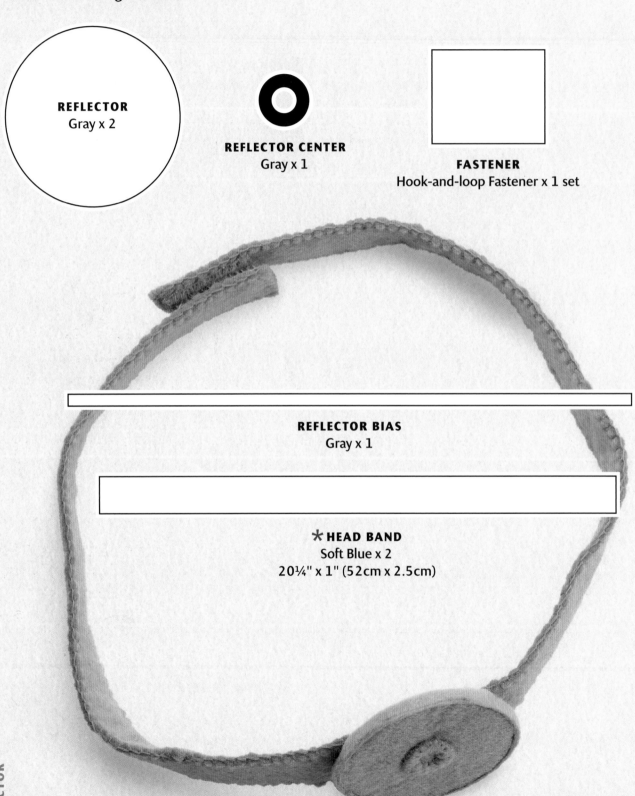

BOTTLE INSIDE
Orange x 1

LABEL
White x 1

BOTTLE OUTSIDE
Orange x 1

Rx

WORDING
Black x 1

BOTTLE CAP SIDE OUTSIDE
White x 1

**BOTTLE
TOP & BASE**
Orange x 2

BOTTLE CAP SIDE INSIDE
White x 1

BOTTLE CAP
White x 1

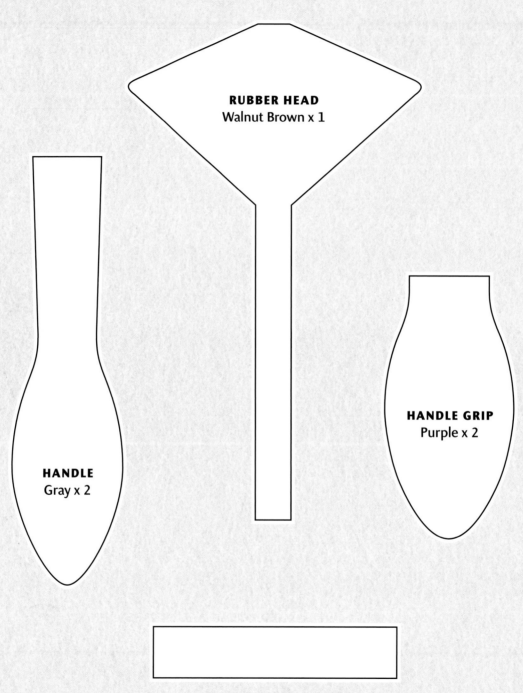

RUBBER HEAD
Walnut Brown x 1

HANDLE
Gray x 2

HANDLE GRIP
Purple x 2

RUBBER HEAD SUPPORT
Gray x 1

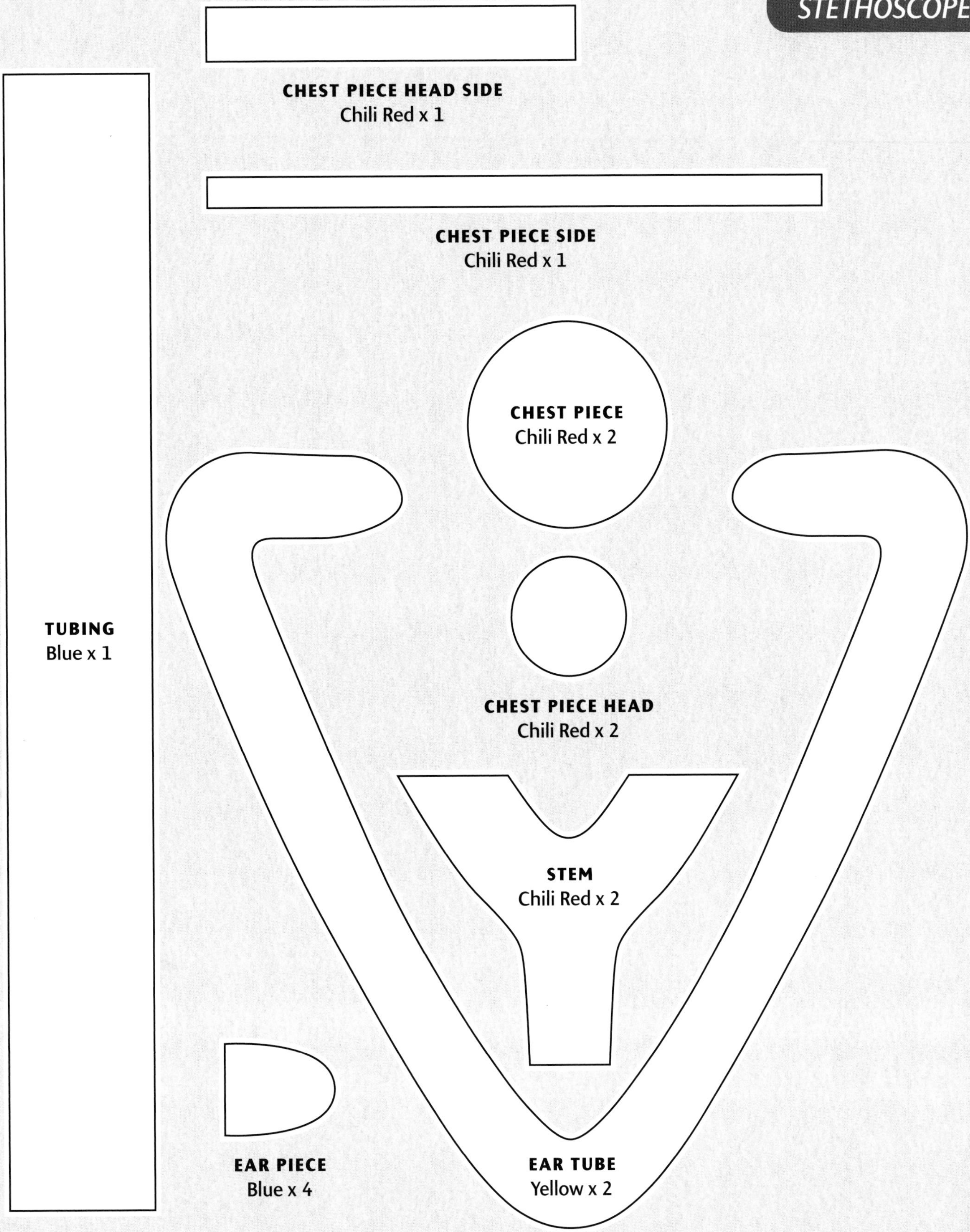

CHEST PIECE HEAD SIDE
Chili Red x 1

CHEST PIECE SIDE
Chili Red x 1

CHEST PIECE
Chili Red x 2

TUBING
Blue x 1

CHEST PIECE HEAD
Chili Red x 2

STEM
Chili Red x 2

EAR PIECE
Blue x 4

EAR TUBE
Yellow x 2

DOCTOR

THUMB REST
Peacock Blue x 2

BARREL BASE
White x 1

PLUNGER TOP & BASE
Peacock Blue x 2

NEEDLE HUB TOP & BASE
Peacock Blue x 2

NEEDLE
Gray x 2

NEEDLE HUB SIDE
Peacock Blue x 1

FINGER FLANGE
White x 2

PLUNGER
Peacock Blue x 1

BARREL INSIDE
White x 1

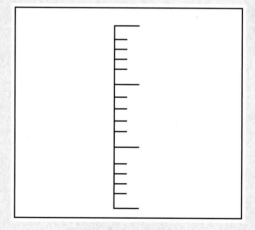

BARREL OUTSIDE
White x 1

BANDAGE
Golden Yellow x 1

BANDAGE CENTER
White x 1

GRILL

Fire up the grill!
Dogs and burgers with all the frills.

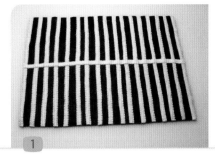

1. Sew the Aluminum grills to the Grill Top, leaving a ⅜" (1cm) interval in between each.

2. Stitch the Grill Sides to the Grill Base.

3. Tape the **cardboard** Grill Sides and the **cardboard** Grill Base together as shown.

4. Insert the cardboard form into the grill.

5. Sew the Grill Top on, leaving an opening for stuffing.

6. Fill the grill with stuffing and then slide the **cardboard** Grill Top piece on top of the filling. Stitch the opening closed.

7. Sew a Grill Leg Side to a Grill Leg Top and Base as shown. Repeat to create the other three legs.

8. Sew the legs onto the base of the grill.

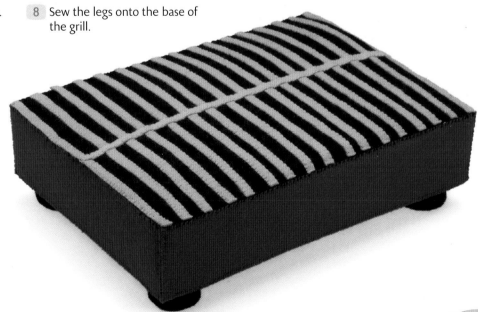

BUN

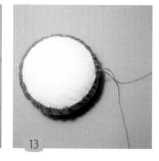

9

10

11

12

13

14

9 Sew the details on the Bun Top. Using a straight stitch, sew 2 to 3mm from the edge of the bun, leaving the thread ends loose.

10 Pull both ends of the threads until the opening matches the Bun Base, and then fasten the threads with knots.

11 Stitch the Bun Base to the Bun Top, leaving an opening for stuffing.

12 Fill the bun with stuffing, and place the **cardboard** Hamburger piece on top of the stuffing as shown.

13 Sew the opening closed.

14 Repeat steps 9 through 13 to make the bottom of the bun (leave out stitching the sesame seeds).

HAMBURGER

15

16

15 Using a backstitch, sew the details on the Hamburger Top and Base.

16 Sew the Hamburger Side to the Hamburger Top and Base, leaving an opening for stuffing. Stuff the burger and stitch up the opening.

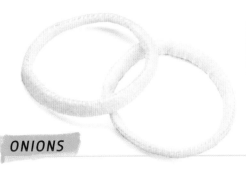
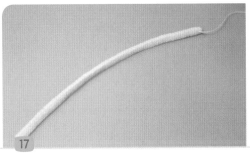

ONIONS

17 Sew the sides of three Onion Ring pieces together.

18 Join and sew the ends together. Shape it into a ring. Repeat for the other onion.

TOMATO SLICES

19 Sew eight Tomato Center pieces to the Tomato Slice as shown.

20 Stitch details on the Centers.

21 Repeat steps 19 and 20 for the other side of the Tomato Slice. Place the slice pieces back to back and sew them together.

LETTUCE

22 Fold the Lettuce Leaf in half and stitch the center vein detail using a backstitch.

23 Fold and sew the other vein details. Turn the lettuce leaf over.

HOT DOG BUN

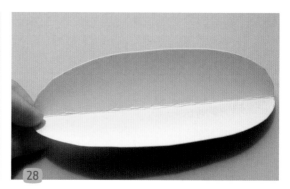

24 Using a backstitch, sew a Bun Side to the Bun Top.

25 Repeat Step 24 for with the other Bun Side.

26 Turn the bun over so the stitches are hidden on the other side.

27 Sew the Bun Base to the Bun Sides, leaving an opening for stuffing.

28 Fold the **cardboard** Bun Top in half. Insert and place it right below the top of the bun.

29 Fill the bun with stuffing.

30 Sew the opening closed.

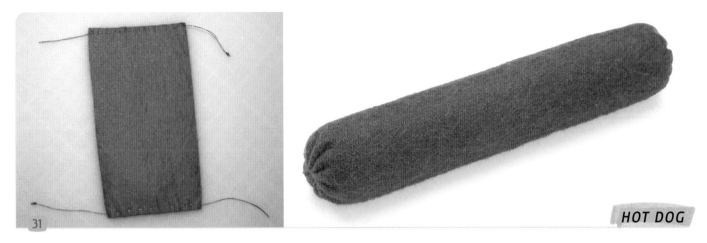

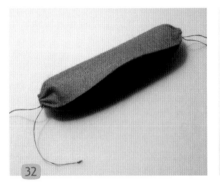

31 Using a straight stitch, stitch 2 to 3mm from the edges of the short ends of the Hot Dog. Leave the threads ends loose as shown.

32 For both ends of the hot dog, pull the threads together, fasten with knots, and trim off the excess threads.

33 Turn the hot dog inside out as shown.

34 Sew the sides together, filling it with stuffing as you sew. Cut out and glue the Mustard Squiggle on top of the hot dog.

CONDIMENT BOTTLE

35

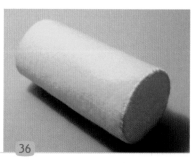

36

37

38

39

40

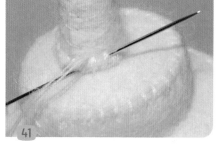

41

35 Sew the sides of the Bottle together.

36 Stitch the Base on.

37 Roll up the PVC plastic sheet and insert into the bottle as shown.

38 Fill the bottle with stuffing and sew the Top on.

39 Sew the Cap Side to the Cap and then stitch it on top of the bottle.

40 Sew the Tip pieces together, fill with stuffing, and sew the Tip Base on.

41 Sew the Tip on top of the Cap.

BLACK
10¼" x 12½" (26cm x 32cm)

BLUE
12" x 14" (30cm x 36cm)

GRAY
7" x 7" (18cm x 18cm)

CHERRY RED
8" x 11" (20cm x 28cm)
4" x 8" (10cm x 20cm)

WHITE
6" x 4¾ (15cm x 12cm)
7" x 4" (18cm x 10cm)

BRIGHT YELLOW
7" x 12" (18cm x 30cm)

GINGERBREAD
8¼" x 10¼" (21cm x 26cm)

COCOA BROWN
4" x 10¼" (10cm x 26cm)

GOLDEN YELLOW
3½" x 3½" (9cm x 9cm)

CHESTNUT BROWN
2¾" x 5" (7cm x 13cm)

LEAF GREEN
4¾" x 4¾" (12cm x 12cm)

MUSTARD YELLOW
5½" x 1½" (14cm x 4cm)

TOMATO RED
10" x 3¼" (25cm x 8cm)

1mm-thick cardboard
11½" x 8¼" (29cm x 21cm),
3 pieces

PVC plastic sheet
8" x 8" (20cm x 20cm)

* Cut out according to measurements stated

* **ALUMINUM GRILL**
Gray x 1
9¾" x ¼" (24.5cm x .5cm)

* **ALUMINUM GRILL**
Gray x 17
7" x ¼" (18cm x .5cm)

* **GRILL TOP**
Black x 1
9¾" x 7" (24.5cm x 18cm)

* **GRILL BASE**
Blue x 1
9¾" x 7" (24.5cm x 18cm)

* **GRILL TOP & BASE**
Cardboard x 2
9" x 6¾" (23.5cm x 17cm)

* **GRILL SIDES**
Blue x 2
9¾" x 2" (24.5cm x 5cm)

* **GRILL SIDES**
Blue x 2
7" x 2" (18cm x 5cm)

* **GRILL SIDES**
Cardboard x 2
9" x 1¾" (23.5cm x 4.5cm)

* **GRILL SIDES**
Cardboard x 2
6¾" x 1¾" (17cm x 4.5cm)

**GRILL LEGS
TOP & BASE**
Black x 8

GRILL LEGS SIDES
Black x 4

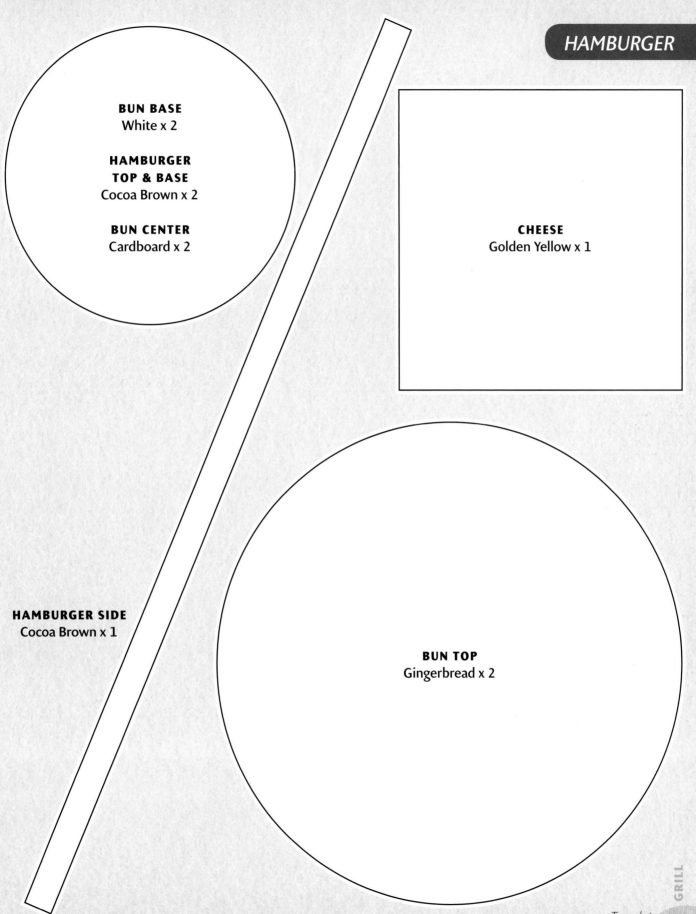

BUN BASE
White x 2

HAMBURGER TOP & BASE
Cocoa Brown x 2

BUN CENTER
Cardboard x 2

CHEESE
Golden Yellow x 1

HAMBURGER SIDE
Cocoa Brown x 1

BUN TOP
Gingerbread x 2

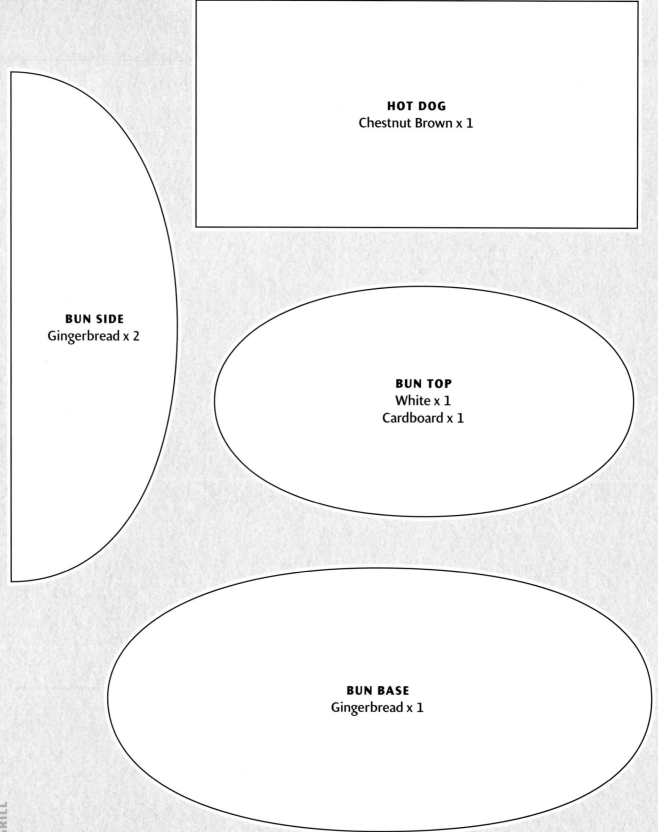

HOT DOG
Chestnut Brown x 1

BUN SIDE
Gingerbread x 2

BUN TOP
White x 1
Cardboard x 1

BUN BASE
Gingerbread x 1

* Cut out according to measurements stated.

KETCHUP & MUSTARD BOTTLE
Cherry Red x 1
Bright Yellow x 1

* **KETCHUP & MUSTARD BOTTLE**
PVC Plastic Sheet x 2
8" x 4" (20cm x 10cm)

KETCHUP & MUSTARD TIP
Cherry Red x 2
Bright Yellow x 2

KETCHUP & MUSTARD
TIP BASE
Cherry Red x 1
Bright Yellow x 1

KETCHUP & MUSTARD CAP SIDE
Cherry Red x 1
Bright Yellow x 1

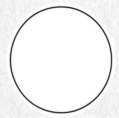

KETCHUP & MUSTARD CAP
Cherry Red x 1
Bright Yellow x 1

KETCHUP & MUSTARD
TOP & BASE
Cherry Red x 2
Bright Yellow x 2

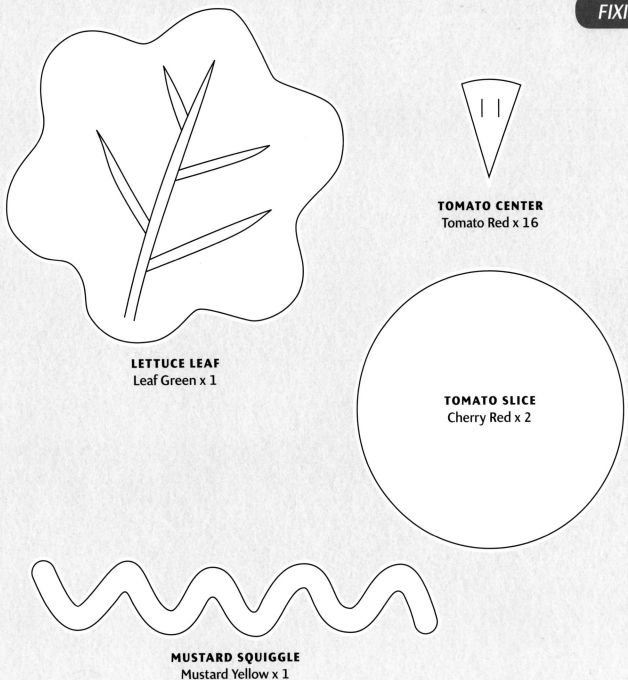

LETTUCE LEAF
Leaf Green x 1

TOMATO CENTER
Tomato Red x 16

TOMATO SLICE
Cherry Red x 2

MUSTARD SQUIGGLE
Mustard Yellow x 1

ONION RINGS
White x 6

PURSE

For the girl on the go, the girl in the know.

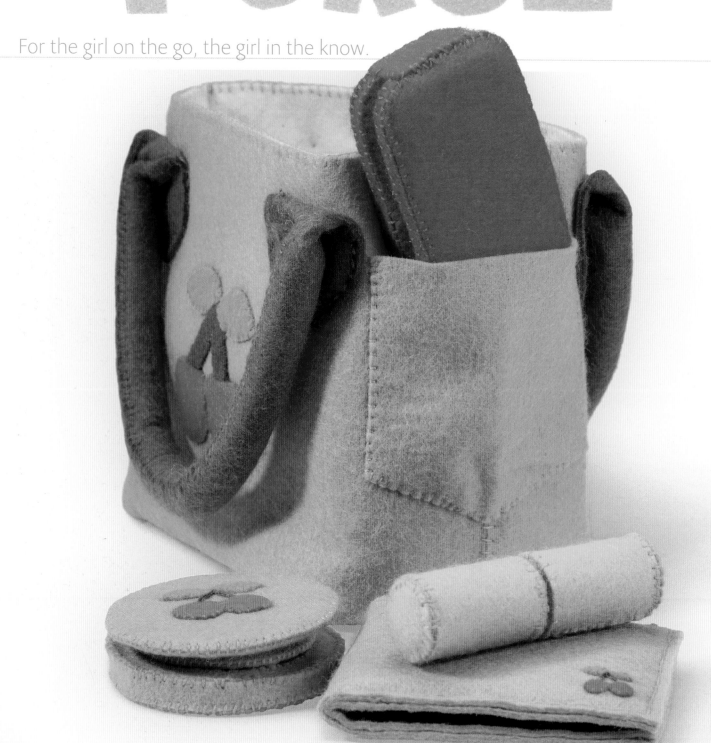

PURSE

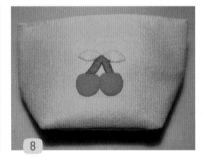

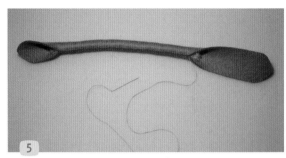

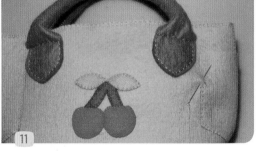

1. Sew the sides of the Outer and Inner Purse together as shown.

2. Turn the purse inside out.

3. Sew the Base to the purse using a backstitch.

4. Turn the purse right side out as shown.

5. Stitch the Handle edges together, leaving the ends unsewn as marked on the pattern. Fill the handles with stuffing as you sew.

6. Repeat the previous step for the other handle.

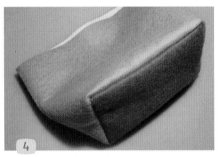

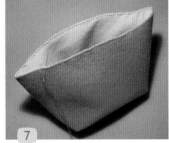

7. Stitch the edge of the purse with a blanket stitch.

8. Sew the Logo pieces onto the center front of the purse as shown.

9. Stitch a handle onto the purse.

10. Repeat for the other handle.

11. Sew the Pockets to each end of the purse as shown.

14

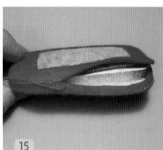

15

16

17

12 Stitch the Numbers onto the Number Keys.

13 Sew the Numbers Keys and Scroll Key onto the Front Casing.

14 Sew the Screen to the Screen Casing.

15 Sew a Casing Side to the Front and Screen Casings, inserting a **cardboard** Casing at the top and bottom, and stuffing in between as shown.

16 Repeat the previous step for the Keypad Casing and Back Casing.

17 Sew the Joint on to the top of both Casings.

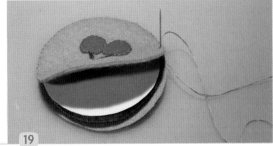

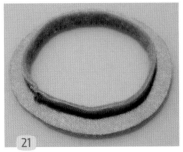

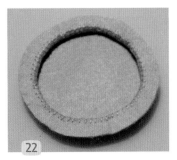

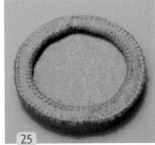

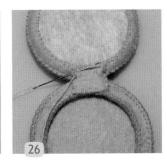

18 Sew the Logo pieces onto the Compact Top, and sew the Mirror to the Mirror Ring.

19 Sandwich a **cardboard** Insert piece in between the Compact Top and Mirror.

20 Sew them together.

21 Sew the Base Inner Side to the Puff Ring.

22 Sew the Inner Base to the Inner Side as shown.

23 Stitch the Outer Side to the Compact Base.

24 Slide a **cardboard** Insert into the base.

25 Sew them together as shown.

26 Sew the Joint to the Mirror and Puff Holder as shown.

27 Sew the Powder Puff pieces together, filling with stuffing. Place the Powder Puff inside the compact.

CREDIT CARD

28 — Sew the Logo onto the Credit Card Top.

29 — Stitch the details on the card as shown.

30 — Sew the Credit Card Top and Base together using a blanket stitch, leaving one end open. Insert the **cardboard** Insert. Stitch the opening closed.

LIPSTICK

31 — Stack and sew the sides of one piece of the Outer Casing and one piece of the Inner Casing together.

32 — Sew the Casing Top and Base (two pieces each) to the Casing, filling it with stuffing (this forms the bottom half of the lipstick tube).

33 — Repeat step 31 and sew the other set of Outer and Inner Casing together, then sew the last two pieces of the Top to one end of the Lipstick Cover.

34 — Finish the open end of the Lipstick Cover with a blanket stitch.

35 — Sew the Center Top and Base to the Center piece filling it with stuffing.

36 — Next sew the Lipstick Top, Lipstick Base, and Lipstick Side together, filling with stuffing as you go.

37 — Sew the Lipstick onto the Center piece.

38 — Then sew it to the Lipstick Casing.

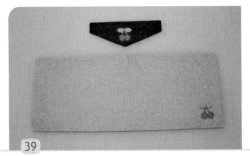

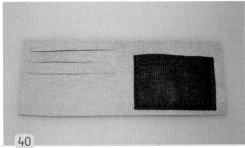

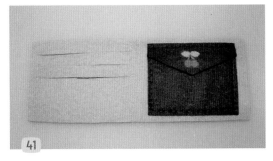

39 Sew the Logo pieces onto the Outer Wallet and Coins Pocket Cover as shown.

40 Sew the Coins Pocket onto the Inner Wallet.

41 Stitch the Coins Pocket Cover in place. Cut slits in the Inner Wallet where indicated on the pattern.

42 Stitch the Inner and Outer Wallet pieces together.

43 Fold the Wallet in half.

LIGHT PURPLE
6" x 7" (15cm x 18cm)

DARK PURPLE
2" x 6¼" (5cm x 16cm)

DARK PINK
2½" x 2½" (6cm x 6cm)

LEAF GREEN
2½" x 2½" (6cm x 6cm)

RASPBERRY PINK
9½" x 14¼" (24cm x 36cm)

PINK
9½" x 11½" (24cm x 30cm)

CHESTNUT BROWN
5½" x 13½" (14cm x 34cm)

WALNUT BROWN
1½" x 2½" (4cm x 6cm)

SOFT PINK
5½" x 5½" (14cm x 14cm)

FADED GRAY
5½" x 3½" (14cm x 9cm)

DEEP PINK
2" x 2" (5cm x 5cm)

BRIGHT YELLOW
3¼" x 4" (8cm x 10cm)

LEMON FROST
2" x 2" (5cm x 5cm)

PEACOCK BLUE
6" x 8" (15cm x 20cm)

SKIN
2" x 4" (5cm x 10cm)

CHILI RED
4" x 8¾" (10cm x 22cm)

WHITE
3¼" x 1½" (8cm x 4cm)

1mm-thick cardboard
11½" x 8¼" (29cm x 21cm)

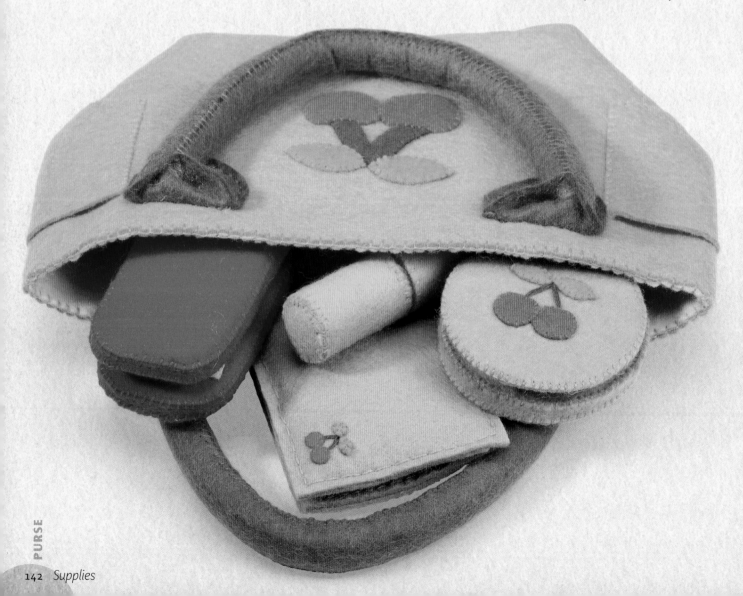

★ OUTER PURSE
Raspberry Pink x 2
9" x 5½" (23cm x 14cm)

★ INNER PURSE
Pink x 2
9" x 5½" (23cm x 14cm)

★ Cut out according to measurements stated

★ BASE
Chestnut Brown x 2
5½" x 3½"
(14cm x 9cm)

POCKET
Raspberry Pink x 2

HANDLE
Chestnut Brown x 2

LOGO (CHERRY)
Dark Pink x 2

LOGO (STEM)
Walnut Brown x 1

LOGO (LEAF)
Leaf Green x 2

Place on fold of fabric and cut

*Cut out according to measurements stated

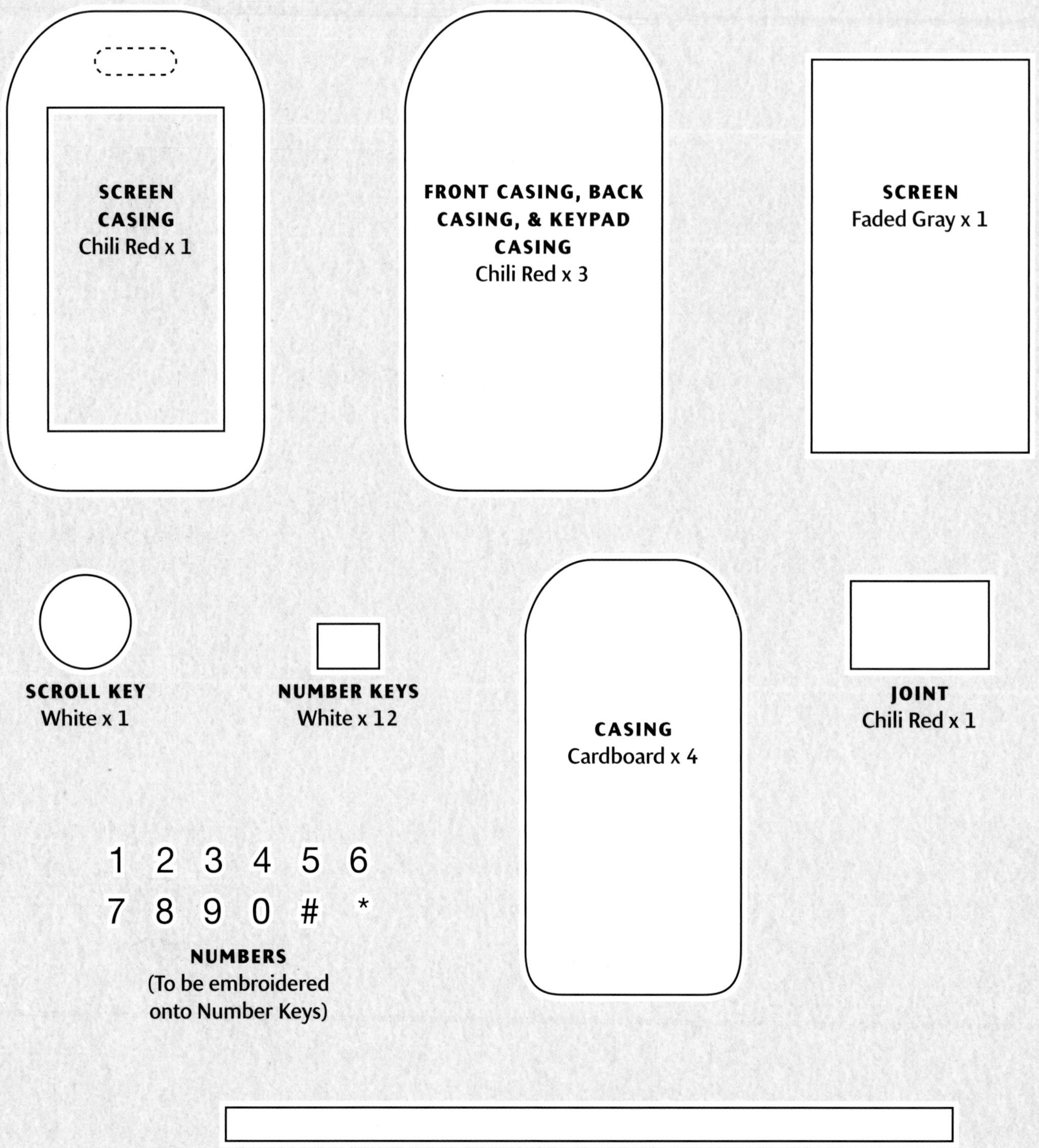

SCREEN
CASING
Chili Red x 1

FRONT CASING, BACK
CASING, & KEYPAD
CASING
Chili Red x 3

SCREEN
Faded Gray x 1

SCROLL KEY
White x 1

NUMBER KEYS
White x 12

CASING
Cardboard x 4

JOINT
Chili Red x 1

1 2 3 4 5 6
7 8 9 0 # *
NUMBERS
(To be embroidered
onto Number Keys)

*CASING SIDES
Chili Red x 2
8½" x ³/₁₆" (21.5cm x .5cm)

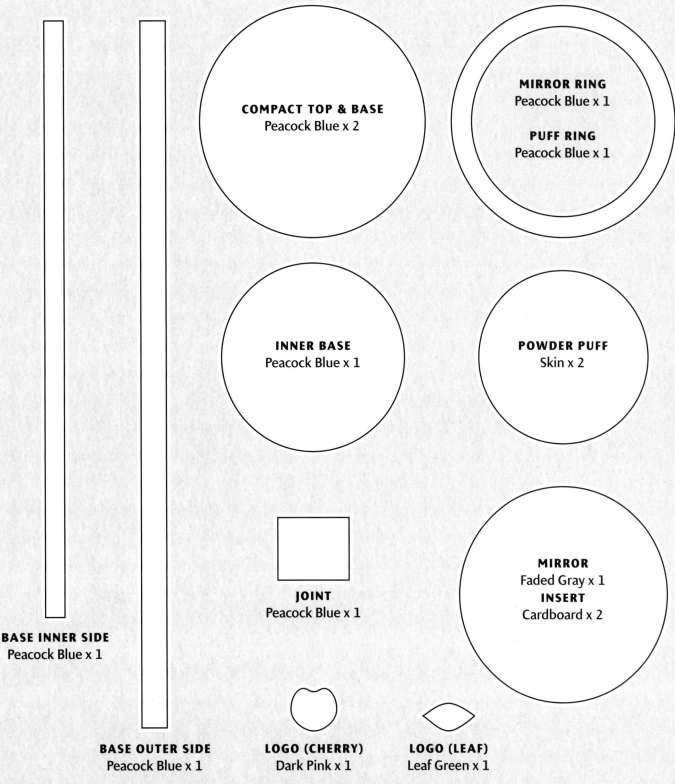

COMPACT TOP & BASE
Peacock Blue x 2

MIRROR RING
Peacock Blue x 1

PUFF RING
Peacock Blue x 1

INNER BASE
Peacock Blue x 1

POWDER PUFF
Skin x 2

JOINT
Peacock Blue x 1

MIRROR
Faded Gray x 1
INSERT
Cardboard x 2

BASE INNER SIDE
Peacock Blue x 1

BASE OUTER SIDE
Peacock Blue x 1

LOGO (CHERRY)
Dark Pink x 1

LOGO (LEAF)
Leaf Green x 1

CREDIT CARD TOP & BASE
Bright Yellow x 2

CREDIT CARD INSERT
Cardboard x 1

**LIPSTICK OUTER CASING
(TOP & BOTTOM)**
Soft Pink x 2

**LIPSTICK INNER CASING
(TOP & BOTTOM)**
Soft Pink x 2

LOGO
Lemon Frost x 1

HOLOGRAM
(To be embroidered
onto card)

Credit Card
0001   4492   7712   5591
Ms Princess

NAME & ACCOUNT NO.
(To be embroidered onto card)

CENTER
Faded Gray x 2

LIPSTICK SIDE
Deep Pink x 1

CASING TOP & BASE
Soft Pink x 6

CENTER TOP & BASE
Faded Gray x 2

LIPSTICK BASE
Deep Pink x 1

LIPSTICK TOP
Deep Pink x 1

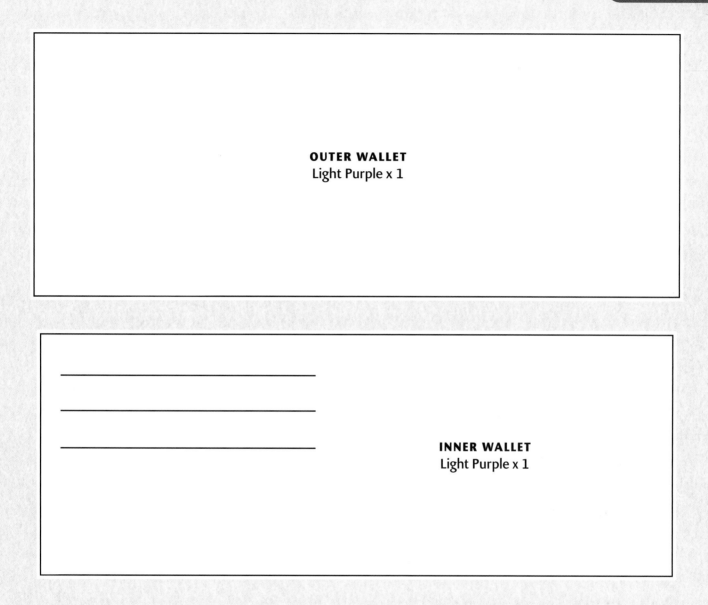

OUTER WALLET
Light Purple x 1

INNER WALLET
Light Purple x 1

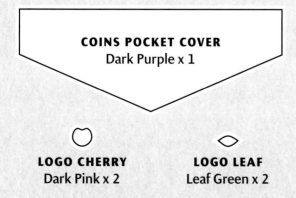

COINS POCKET COVER
Dark Purple x 1

COINS POCKET
Dark Purple x 1

LOGO CHERRY
Dark Pink x 2

LOGO LEAF
Leaf Green x 2

PURSE

FRUITS

Half for me, half for you.
(Magnets hold it together, too.)

WATERMELON

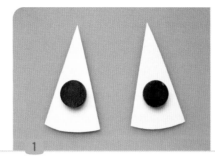

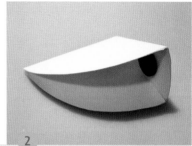

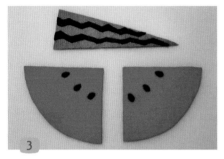

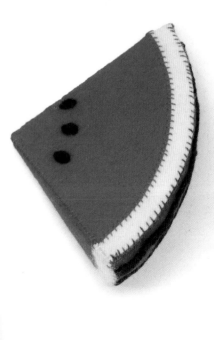

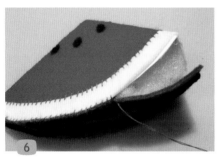

1. Glue the Magnet Buttons on the wrong side of the **cardboard** Watermelon Center pieces, making sure that when you place the right sides of both cardboards together, the magnets attract and not repel.

2. Tape the **cardboard** Watermelon Front, Back, and Center pieces together as shown.

3. Sew the details onto the Watermelon Front, Back, and Skin as shown.

4. Stitch the Watermelon Rind pieces to the Watermelon as shown.

5. Sew all three pieces together.

6. Insert the cardboard form inside the Watermelon, and fill with stuffing.

7. Sew the Skin to the Watermelon.

8. Repeat the same for the other watermelon half.

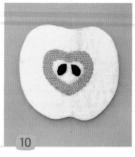

APPLE

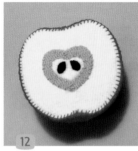

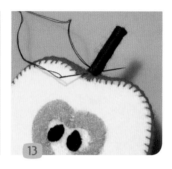

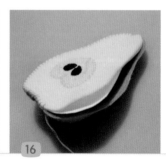

9   Sew three Apple Skin pieces together.

10   Sew the Apple Seeds and the Apple Center hook-and-loop fasteners to the Apple Inside as shown.

11   Sew the Apple Skin and Apple Inside halfway, insert the **cardboard** Apple Base, and fill with stuffing.

12   Seal up the opening and repeat the same for the other half of the Apple.

13   Roll the Apple Stalk and sew it on top of one of the Apple halves as shown.

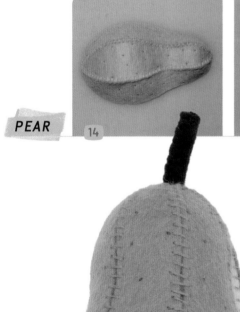

PEAR

14   Sew three Pear Skin sides together, then stitch the details on the skin using brown thread.

15   Sew the Pear Seeds and the Pear Center hook-and-loop fasteners onto the center of the Pear Inside as shown.

16   Sew the Pear Inside to the Skin halfway, insert the **cardboard** Pear Base, and fill with stuffing. Stitch the opening closed. Repeat the same for the other half.

17   Roll up the Pear Stalk and sew it on top of one of the Pear halves as shown.

KIWI

18

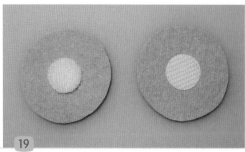
19

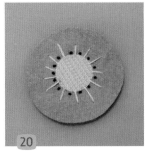
20

21

22

23

18 Sew six Kiwi Skins together.

19 Sew hook-and-loop fasteners onto the Kiwi Center.

20 Stitch the details on the Kiwi Center as shown.

21 Sew the Kiwi Center and the Skin together halfway, insert the **cardboard** Kiwi Base, fill with stuffing, and sew shut.

22 Sew the Stalk on top of the Kiwi.

23 Repeat the same for the other half.

BANANA

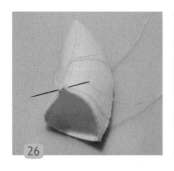  

24 Glue the Magnet Buttons onto the wrong side of the **cardboard** Banana Bases, making certain that the cardboard attracts and not repels when the right sides are placed together.

25 Stitch the details on the Banana Center as shown.

26 Sew a Banana Top and two Banana Sides together as shown.

27 Sew the Center and the Banana together halfway, and insert the **cardboard** Base. Fill with stuffing and then stitch the opening closed.

28 Repeat the same for the other Banana half.

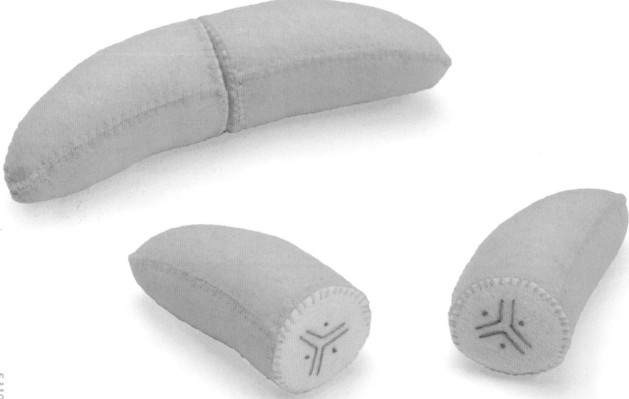

FRUIT KNIFE

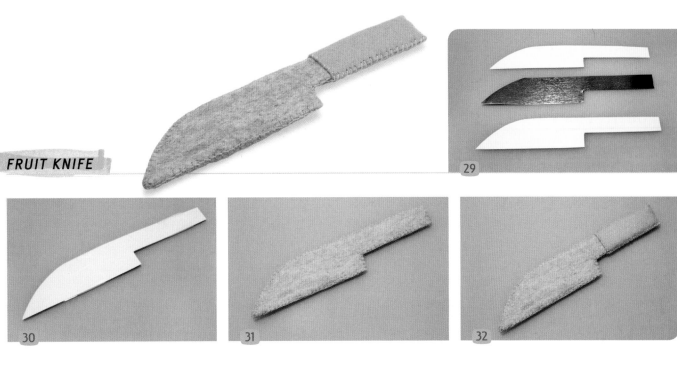

29 Place the Metal Sheet Knife Base in between the two **cardboard** pieces of the Fruit Knife.

30 Tape them together.

31 Place the taped Base in between the two pieces of the felt Fruit Knife, and sew them together.

32 Wrap and sew the Handle onto the Knife as shown.

CUTTING BOARD

33 Sew the two Cutting Board pieces together, leaving the top open. Insert the three **cardboard** Base pieces and stitch the opening closed.

FRUITS

BABY PINK
6" x 8¼" (15cm x 21cm)

BRIGHT YELLOW
6¼" x 7" (16cm x 18cm)

LEMON FROST
5" x 8" (13cm x 20cm)

LEAF GREEN
2" x 4" (5cm x 10cm)

WALNUT BROWN
¾" x 1½" (2cm x 4cm)

GINGERBREAD
4" x 7" (10cm x 18cm)

FADED GRAY
3¼" x 6¼" (8cm x 16cm)

SKY BLUE
2" x 2½" (5cm x 6cm)

GREEN TEA
4¾" x 8" (12cm x 20cm)

BLACK
1½" x 4¾" (4cm x 12cm)

COCOA BROWN
1¼" x ¾" (3cm x 2cm)

CHILI RED
7" x 15¾" (18cm x 40cm)

IVORY
4¾" x 6¼" (12cm x 16cm)

GREEN
4" x 4¾" (10cm x 12cm)

25mm magnet buttons
4 pieces

Beige hook-and-loop fastener
¾" x 2½" (2cm x 6cm)

Skin hook-and-loop fastener
¾" x 2½" (2cm x 6cm)

White hook-and-loop fastener
¾" x 2½" (2cm x 6cm)

0.008 tin sheet metal
1¼" x 6" (3cm x 15cm)

1mm-thick cardboard
23¼" x 16½" (59cm x 42cm),
2 pieces

Wire cutters

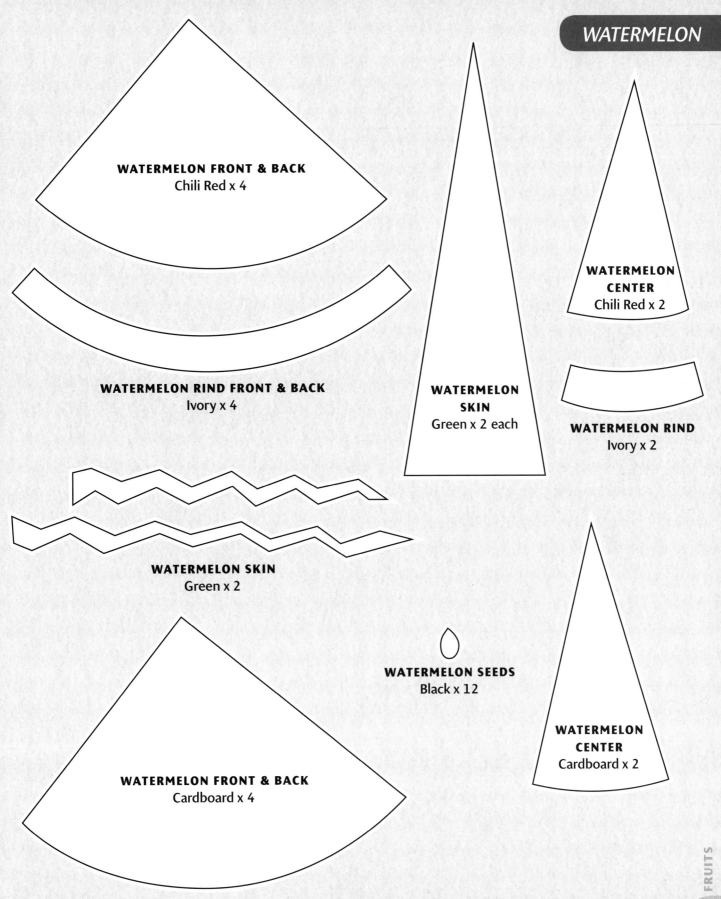

WATERMELON FRONT & BACK
Chili Red x 4

WATERMELON RIND FRONT & BACK
Ivory x 4

WATERMELON CENTER
Chili Red x 2

WATERMELON SKIN
Green x 2 each

WATERMELON RIND
Ivory x 2

WATERMELON SKIN
Green x 2

WATERMELON SEEDS
Black x 12

WATERMELON FRONT & BACK
Cardboard x 4

WATERMELON CENTER
Cardboard x 2

FRUITS

PEAR INSIDE
Lemon Frost x 2

PEAR BASE
Cardboard x 2

PEAR SKIN
Green Tea x 6

APPLE SEEDS
Black x 4
PEAR SEEDS
Black x 4

APPLE CENTER
Beige Hook-and-loop fasteners x 4
(2 hooks sides, 2 loops sides)
PEAR CENTER
Skintone Hook-and-loop fasteners x 4
(2 hooks sides, 2 loops sides)

APPLE STALK
Cocoa Brown x 1
PEAR STALK
Cocoa Brown x 1

APPLE INSIDE
Lemon Frost x 2

APPLE BASE
Cardboard x 2

APPLE SKIN
Chili Red x 6

BANANA SIDES
Bright Yellow x 4

BANANA TOP
Bright Yellow x 2

KIWI SKIN
Gingerbread x 12

BANANA CENTER
Lemon Frost x 2

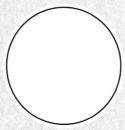

BANANA BASE
Cardboard x 2

KIWI CENTER
White Hook-and-loop
fastener x 1 set

KIWI STALK
Walnut Brown x 2

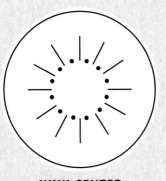

KIWI CENTER
Leaf Green x 2

KIWI BASE
Cardboard x 2

FRUIT KNIFE HANDLE
Sky Blue x 1

FRUIT KNIFE
Faded Gray x 2

FRUIT KNIFE BASE
Cardboard x 2
.008cm Metal Sheet x 1

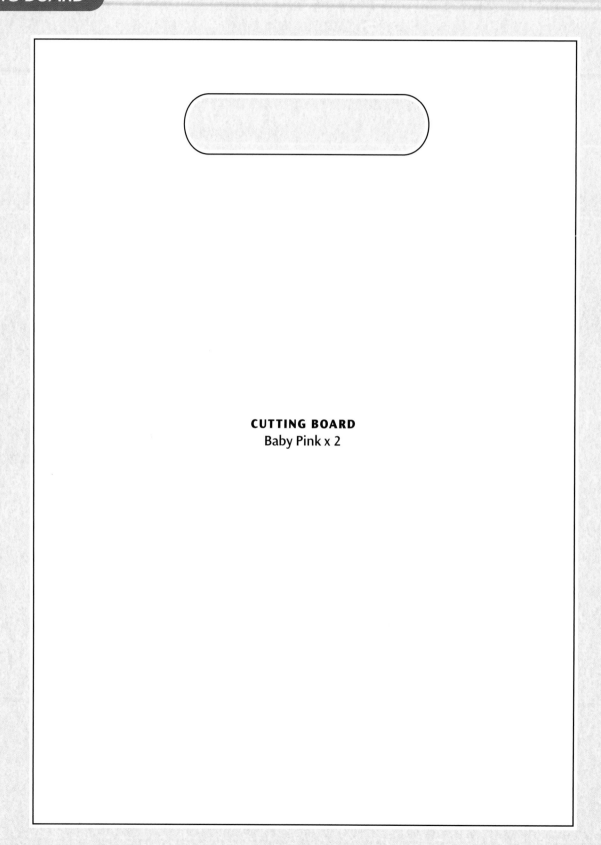

CUTTING BOARD
Baby Pink x 2

CUTTING BOARD BASE
Cardboard x 3

TOOLS

Build it! Fix it! Wear it! Share it!

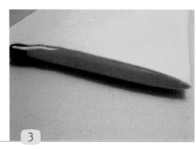

TOOL BELT

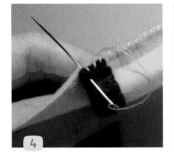
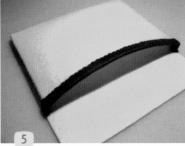
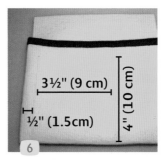
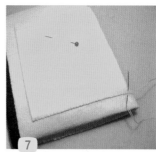

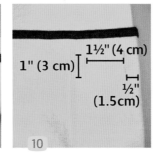

3½" (9 cm)
½" (1.5cm)
4" (10 cm)

1" (3 cm)
1½" (4 cm)
½" (1.5cm)

1. Fold the Big Pocket Bias in half and sew it to the big pocket as shown.

2. Fold the sides of the Big Pocket in as shown.

3. Fold the big pocket up to the fold line indicated on the pattern.

4. Sew the sides together.

5. Your Big Pocket should look like this at this stage.

6. Draw two parellel lines on the big pocket according to the measurements as shown.

7. Pin down and sew the Small Pocket to the line.

8. Repeat the same for the other side (note: there will be "extra" felt).

9. Fold both sides of the small pocket and sew the bottom on as shown.

10. Draw two more parellel lines according to measurement as shown.

11. Sew the sides of the Hammer Holder as shown.

12. Fold the Belt Slot in half and pin it to the top of the big pocket as shown. Sew the Belt Slot on. Insert a belt into the Belt Slot.

DRILL

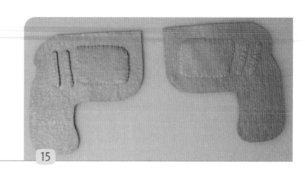

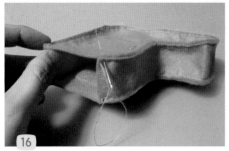

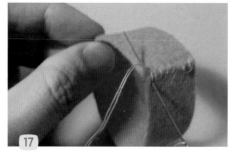

15 Sew the Fan Coolers to the Drill Housings as shown.

16 Using a backstitch, sew the Drill Housing Side to the wrong-side of the Drill Housings.

17 Sew the sides of the Drill Collar together.

18 Insert the Drill Collar into the opening of the drill as shown.

19 Stitch them together with a backstitch.

20 Turn the drill inside out and stuff it.

21 Sew the Collar Front to the Collar.

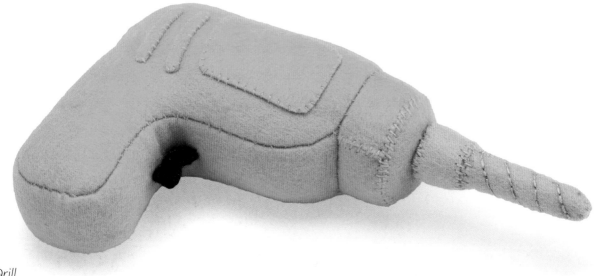

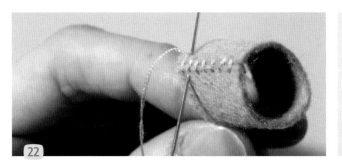

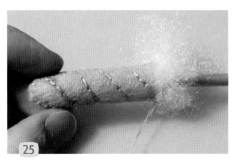

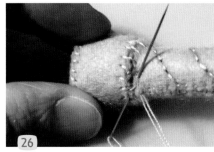

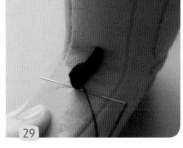

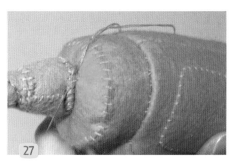

22 Sew the sides of the Rotor Side together.

23 Sew the Rotor Base to the Rotor Side, stuff it, then sew the Rotor Top on.

24 Using a backstitch, stitch the details onto the Drill Bit as shown.

25 Sew the Drill Bit sides together, then stuff the piece.

26 Sew the Bit to the Rotor.

27 Stitch the Rotor onto the Collar.

28 Sew the two pieces of the Switch together.

29 Sew the Switch onto the center of the Drill.

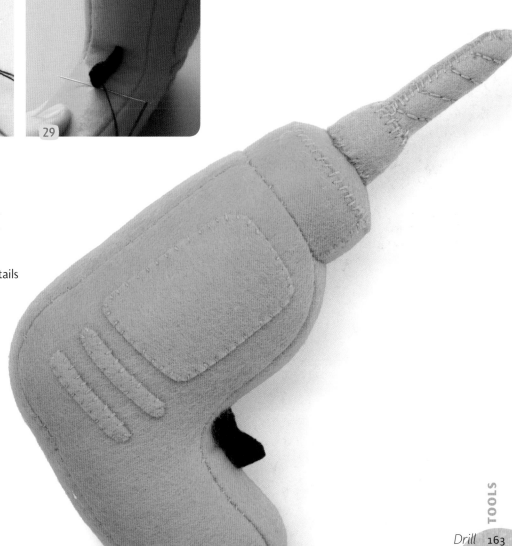

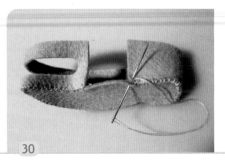
30

31

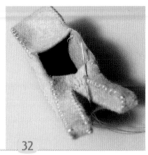
32

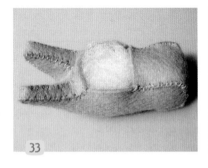
33

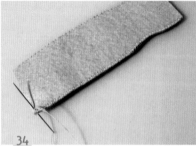
34

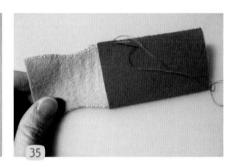
35

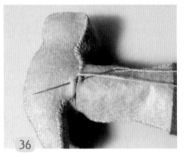
36

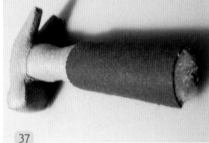
37

38

30 Sew the Hammer Head and Hammer Head Side together.

31 Repeat on the other side.

32 Sew the Hammer Claw onto the center as shown.

33 Fill the hammer head with stuffing.

34 Sew the two Hammer Body pieces together.

35 Wrap and sew the Handle onto the body.

36 Sew the body onto the hammer head as shown.

37 Fill the Handle with stuffing.

38 Sew on the Handle Base.

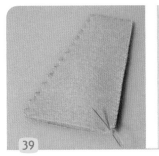
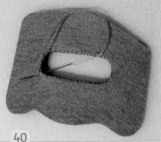

39 Sew the two Blades together, leaving the top open as shown.

40 Sew the inner part of the Handle together.

41 Sew the outer part of the Handle together.

42 Fill the Handle with stuffing as you sew.

43 Leave an opening at one side as shown.

44 Insert the **cardboard** Blade in between the felt blades.

45 Sew the blade and handle together as shown.

46

47

48

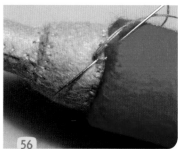

49

50

51

52

53

54

55

56

46 Sew the two Blade pieces together, leaving an opening as shown.

47 Stitch the sides of the Chuck Side together.

48 Sew on the Chuck Top and Chuck Base, leaving an opening for stuffing.

49 Fill the Chuck with stuffing and sew up the opening.

50 Fill the Blade with stuffing.

51 Sew the Blade and Chuck together as shown.

52 Stitch the sides of the Handle together.

53 Sew on the Handle Top.

54 Sew the Handle Base base on, leaving an opening for stuffing.

55 Fill the Handle with stuffing and sew the opening closed.

56 Sew the Handle to the Chuck.

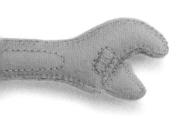

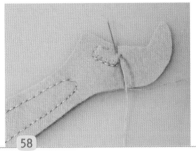

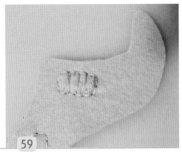

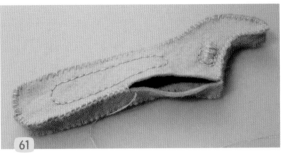

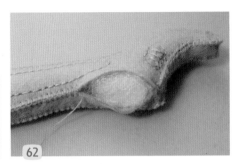

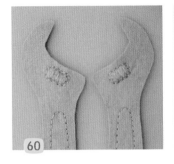

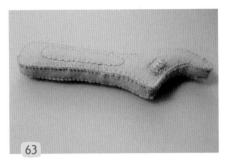

57 Stitch the details onto the Wrenches as shown.

58 Sew the Adjuster onto the Wrench.

59 Sew the details on the Adjuster.

60 Repeat the same for both sides.

61 Sew the Big Wrench Side to the Wrench, leaving an opening for stuffing.

62 Fill the wrench with stuffing.

63 Sew the opening closed.

64 Sew the Small Wrench Side to the Small Wrench, leaving an opening for stuffing.

65 Fill the Small Wrench with stuffing and sew the opening shut.

66 Sew the Small Wrench onto the Big Wrench as shown.

YELLOW
8¾" x 11½" (22cm x 30cm)

CHESTNUT BROWN
3½" x 6¼" (9cm x 16cm)

ORANGE
13½" x 6" (34cm x 15cm)

WALNUT BROWN
8¾" x 6¼" (22cm x 16cm)

GRAY
11½" x 15¾" (30cm x 40cm)

BLACK
1¼" x 1½" (3cm x 4cm)

CHILI RED
4" x 4¼" (10cm x 11cm)

BLUE
4" x 4¾" (10cm x 12cm)

1mm-thick cardboard
4¾" x 5½" (12cm x 14cm)

* Cut out according to measurements stated

– – – – Indicates fold

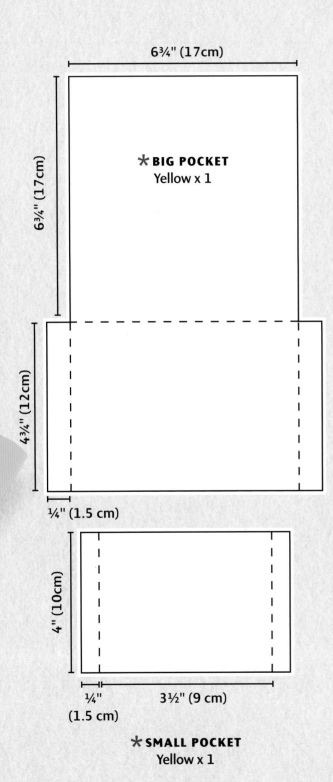

6¾" (17cm)

6¾" (17cm)

***BIG POCKET**
Yellow x 1

4¾" (12cm)

¼" (1.5 cm)

4" (10cm)

¼"
(1.5 cm)   3½" (9 cm)

***SMALL POCKET**
Yellow x 1

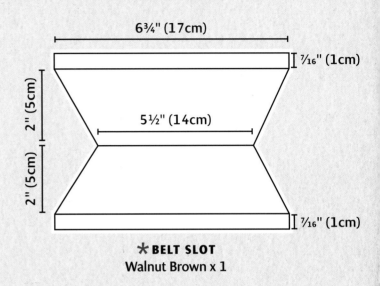

6¾" (17cm)

⁷⁄₁₆" (1cm)

2" (5cm)

5½" (14cm)

2" (5cm)

⁷⁄₁₆" (1cm)

***BELT SLOT**
Walnut Brown x 1

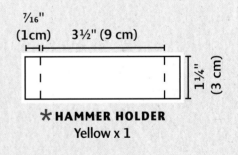

⁷⁄₁₆"
(1cm)   3½" (9 cm)

1¼"
(3 cm)

***HAMMER HOLDER**
Yellow x 1

***BIG POCKET BIAS**
Walnut Brown x 1
8" x ¾" (20cm x 2cm)

* Cut out according to measurements stated

– – – — Indicates Sewing Lines

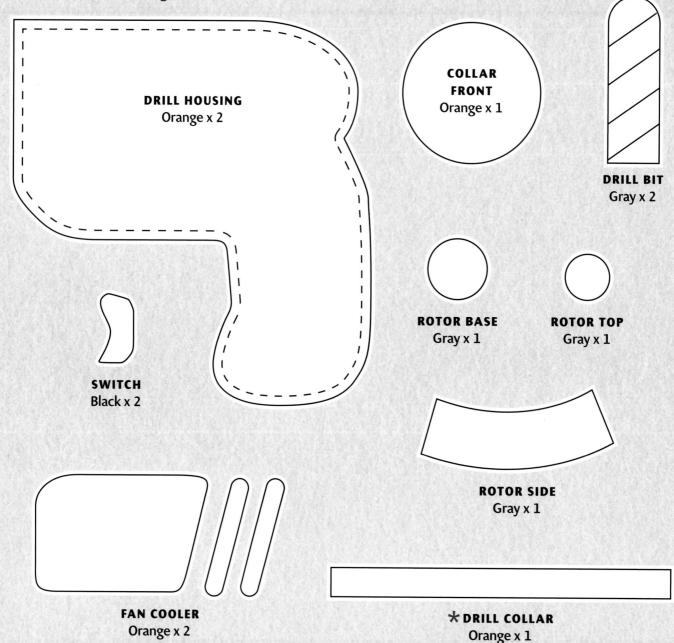

DRILL HOUSING
Orange x 2

COLLAR FRONT
Orange x 1

DRILL BIT
Gray x 2

SWITCH
Black x 2

ROTOR BASE
Gray x 1

ROTOR TOP
Gray x 1

ROTOR SIDE
Gray x 1

FAN COOLER
Orange x 2

＊DRILL COLLAR
Orange x 1
4¾" x ¾" (12cm x 2cm)

＊DRILL HOUSING SIDE
Orange x 1
12¾" x 1¼" (32.7cm x 3cm)

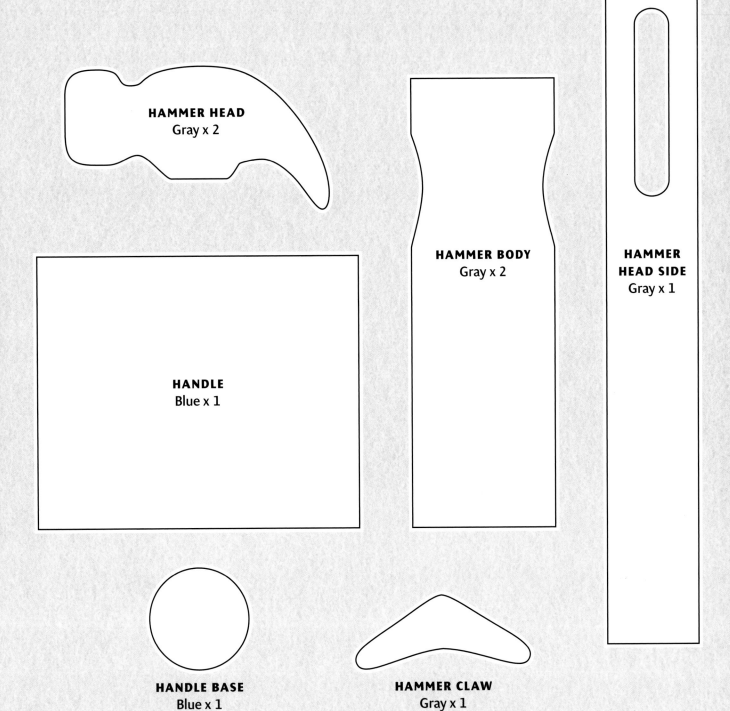

HAMMER HEAD
Gray x 2

HAMMER BODY
Gray x 2

**HAMMER
HEAD SIDE**
Gray x 1

HANDLE
Blue x 1

HANDLE BASE
Blue x 1

HAMMER CLAW
Gray x 1

TOOLS

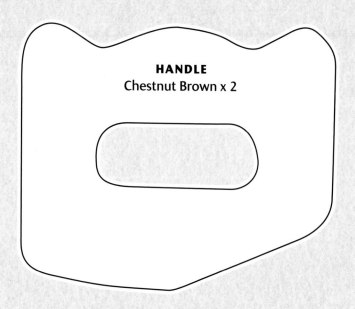

HANDLE
Chestnut Brown x 2

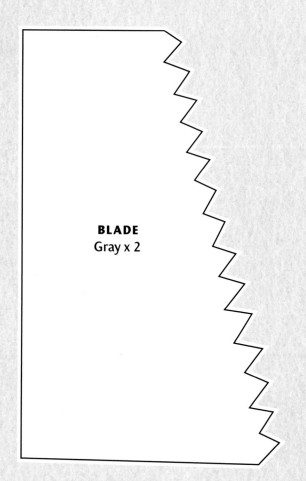

BLADE
Gray x 2

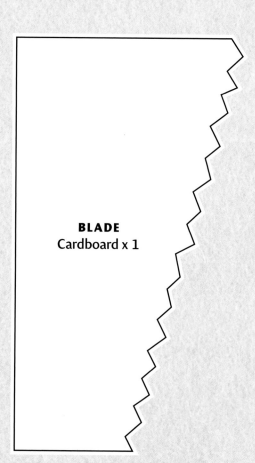

BLADE
Cardboard x 1

BLADE
Gray x 2

CHUCK SIDE
Gray x 1

CHUCK BASE
Gray x 1

CHUCK TOP
Gray x 1

HANDLE
Chili Red x 1

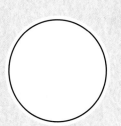

HANDLE TOP & BASE
Chili Red x 2

TOOLS

* Cut out according to measurements stated

SMALL WRENCH
Gray x 2

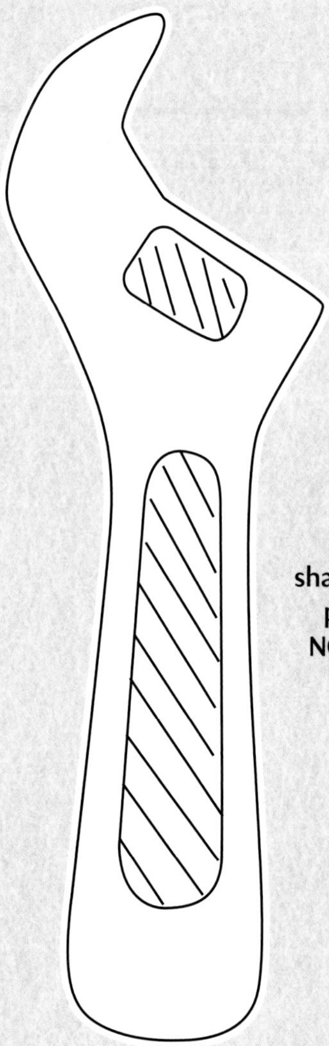

WRENCH
Gray x 2
(NOTE: Cut out
shaded area on paper
pattern only and
NOT on felt fabrics)

ADJUSTER
Gray x 2

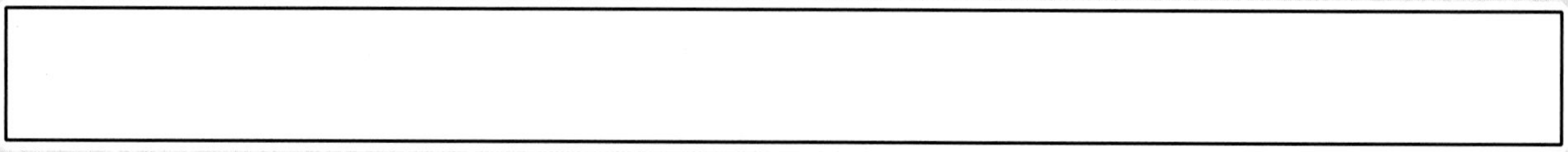

***BIG WRENCH SIDE**
Gray x 1
12½" x ⁷⁄₁₆" (32cm x 1cm)

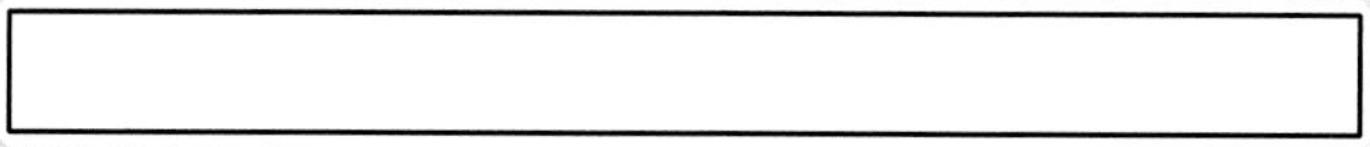

***SMALL WRENCH SIDE**
Gray x 1
2¾" x ⁷⁄₁₆" (7cm x 1cm)

Jeanette Lim is a designer, visualist, and creative thinker with a passion for crafts. Inspired by a book on felt food, she began making felt doughnuts and cupcakes in early 2008 during a difficult pregnancy that prevented her from working outside the home. Since then she has sold over 6,000 of her own original patterns in her Etsy shop (umecrafts.etsy.com). While many of her sales are to crafters in the U.S. and the U.K., she has customers all over the world. Besides selling her original patterns, she has filled numerous custom order requests from stay-at-home moms, young professionals, and grandmothers. Jeanette is one of the 12 featured crafters in *Craft-In* (Lark Crafts, 2010). She lives in Singapore.

acknowledgments

I would like to thank SunFelt Co. Ltd. for generously supplying me with the felt used in the projects, and to thank my editor, Linda Kopp, for this wonderful opportunity and for being so patient.

index